QUICK & EASY DIABETIC COOKBOOK FOR BEGINNERS

Eat Well, Live Better: Lots of Flavorful, Low-Sugar & Low-Carb Recipes for Type 2 Diabetes and Prediabetes.
Incl. 30-Day Meal Plan & Weekly Shopping List

Natalie A. Sullivan

Table Of Contents

INTRODUCTION

Have you ever wondered about what it is like to find out you have diabetes? To hear those three words from your doctor, "You have diabetes." It is a moment that can send a shiver down your spine. And fill your mind with countless questions. What does this mean for your future? What can you eat? What should you avoid? How will your life change? Getting diabetes can feel like a challenge. But here is the good news. You are not certainly alone in this journey. You have just picked up a copy of the "Instant & Easy Diabetic Cookbook for Beginners," and I am here to guide you. To show you that living with diabetes can be not just manageable but also enjoyable.

Getting diagnosed with diabetes can be overwhelming. It is like being handed a puzzle with missing pieces and no instruction manual. The questions race through your mind and you might find yourself feeling scared and anxious. You may wonder if you will have to give up all your favorite foods, whether life will be a never-ending cycle of needles and medications, or if you will ever be able to enjoy a sweet treat again. But let's take a deep breath and slow down. It is true that diabetes is a serious condition, but it doesn't have to be as frightening as it might seem at first. It is not about what you cannot do or cannot eat. It is about finding new ways to enjoy your life while managing your condition.

How one gets it?

In your body, there is a special helper called insulin. It is like the key that unlocks the door for glucose to enter your cells. This process is crucial because it allows your body to use glucose for energy. Sometimes, things can go wrong. When you eat too much sugar or unhealthy foods regularly, your body may have more glucose than it can handle. It is like overloading the car with too much fuel. To manage this excess glucose, your pancreas, a small-sized organ in your belly, works hard to make extra insulin.

Over time, if you keep overloading your body with sugar and not being active enough, your cells can become "insulin resistant." It is like your cells have stubborn locks that the insulin key doesn't fit anymore. This means the glucose can't enter your cells and it stays in your blood, which causes high blood sugar levels. Your genes can also play a role. If diabetes runs in your family, your risk of getting it may be higher. Think of it as having a family history of car trouble. However, you can still make choices to reduce your risk.

Before diabetes develops, there is a stage called prediabetes. It is a bit like a warning sign. During prediabetes, your blood sugar levels consistently stay higher than normal, but not high enough to cause diabetes. It is a chance to make changes and prevent diabetes from taking hold. For some women, pregnancy can bring a condition called gestational diabetes. It is only temporary. During pregnancy, in some cases body of a woman fails to make enough insulin to metabolize the glucose and that leads to higher blood sugar levels. After giving birth this form of diabetes ceases to exist, but it is essential to keep an eye on it and prevent it from causing any serious damage to the health of the mother and the child. When it comes to diabetes there is always a reason behind its cause. Sometimes it is the combination of various factors that work together and cause the disease, such as consuming an unhealthy diet, being inactive and having a genetic tendency. It is important to understand how these factors can create an impact so that we can take effective measures to prevent or manage the disease.

The Vital Role of Balanced Nutrition in Diabetes Management

When it comes to diabetes management, a healthy diet plays a supreme role. The amount of food especially the carbs we consume is directly related to the blood sugar level. So, it is important to carefully consider what to eat and in how much amount, if you are having diabetes. Whether it is Type 1 or Type 2, in diabetes body loses the ability to regulate normal blood sugar levels. Nutrition plays a crucial role in controlling these levels, thus preventing complications and maintaining overall health.
A well-balanced diet can help control blood sugar levels and prevent the dangerous glucose spikes which lead to diabetic emergencies. It is crucial to monitor carbohydrate intake, as they have a direct impact on blood sugar. A diet rich in complex carbohydrates and fiber and low in simple sugars can help in maintaining steady glucose levels. The right nutrition can help in weight management, which is particularly important for those with Type 2 diabetes. It is equally important to keep a healthy body weight to reduce insulin resistance and decrease the risk of further health issues.

Balanced nutrition also supports heart health as well. People with diabetes are at higher risk of cardiovascular problems. A diet low in saturated fats, salt and cholesterol can help manage this risk. Proper nutrition can improve overall well-being. Nutrient-rich foods provide essential vitamins and minerals that improves the immune system, increase energy levels and contribute to a better quality of life.
Starting a new diet can be a bit difficult. There will be twists and turns. The key is not to give up if things get challenging. Just like in any journey, there will be bumps in the road, but with determination and a positive attitude, you can overcome them. Rome wasn't built in a day and same is true for healthy eating habits. Take one step at a time and soon you will find that your new diet becomes a natural part of your life. It is all about making sustainable changes that will benefit your health in the long run.

CHAPTER 1: What is Diabetes-type 2?

It is a condition in which your body strives to manage blood sugar levels. Our bodies break down the food we eat into sugar, which is our main source of energy. But, to get this sugar from your blood into your cells where it is needed, your body uses a hormone called insulin. In type 2 diabetes, something goes a little haywire with this system. Unlike type 1 diabetes, where your body does not make any insulin at all, in type 2 the body produces insulin. However, it is not done effectively, as the body does not make enough insulin. This leads to higher levels of sugar in the blood, which isn't good for your health.

Differences from Other Types of Diabetes

Now, you might have heard of other types of diabetes like type 1 or gestational diabetes. The type 1 often makes its appearance during childhood or adolescence, though it can occur at any age. It happens when your body's immune system, the superhero that mostly fights off illness, turns against the pancreas. Your pancreas, which is like a control center for managing your blood sugar, stops producing insulin, a hormone essential for regulating your sugar levels.

Without insulin, your blood sugar levels skyrocket. This means you will need to inject insulin daily, or use an insulin pump to keep your blood sugar in check. You will also need to be mindful of what you eat, exercise and how your body responds to insulin. While it can be challenging, remember that there are several people with diabetes who are living active, fulfilling lives.

On the other hand, gestational diabetes appears during pregnancy and, for most women, goes away after giving birth. It happens when the body can't produce insulin enough to meet the needs of the body during pregnancy. While it is temporary, it is essential to manage it carefully to ensure the well-being of both mom and baby.

Prediabetes

It is like a warning sign from your body that your blood sugar levels are consistently than they should be and you need to take effective measures to stop it from progressing. If you have prediabetes, it is your body's way of saying, "Let's make some changes before things get more serious." The good news is that with lifestyle adjustments, such as a healthier diet and increased physical activity, you can often prevent or delay the progression to full-blown diabetes. Think of it as an opportunity to take control of your health and well-being.

Symptoms of Type 2 Diabetes

Type 2 can be sneaky and develop over time. You might not even notice any symptoms at first. But, as it slowly progresses, some signs and symptoms may show up. If you experience any of these, it is essential to discuss with your doctor:

- Excessive Urination: You might find yourself making more trips to the bathroom, especially at night. This happens because your kidneys are trying to get rid of the excess sugar in your blood through your urine.
- More Thirst: All that urination can make you super thirsty. Your body needs more fluids to replace the ones you are losing.
- Constant Fatigue: High blood sugar levels can make you feel tired and sluggish because your cells aren't getting the energy they need.
- Compromised Vision: When your blood sugar levels are high, it can affect the lenses in your eyes, and cause blurry vision.
- Slow Healing of Wounds: This is a common symptom of diabetes. The wounds do not heal quickly and diabetics need to take extra care of the wounds.
- Sense of Tingling or Numbness: High levels of sugar can hit the nerves and that lead to a tingling sensation or numbness.
- Unexpected Weight Loss: This happens because your body isn't effectively using the calories from the food you eat.
- Repeated Infections: High sugar levels can weaken your immune system, making you more prone to infections like yeast infections.

Diagnosing Type 2 Diabetes

If you notice any of the symptoms I have mentioned above, or if you have risk factors like a family history of diabetes, it is essential to consult a health specialist or a doctor. They can perform tests to diagnose type 2 diabetes. Here is what you can expect:

- Fasting Blood Sugar Test: This test is used to measure the blood sugar level after fasting for 12 hours. If the glucose is measured to be 126 milligrams per deciliter (mg/dL) or higher on this test which indicates diabetes.
- A1C Test: Through this test the average blood glucose levels over the past 2-3months are measured. If the result is 6.5% or higher then it shows that the patient has diabetes.
- Oral Glucose Tolerance Test (OGTT): This test is used to measure the glucose levels after an overnight fast and then making the patient drink sugary solution before the test. After regular intervals the blood sugar levels are measured. If the result turns out to be 200 mg/dL or higher after two hours of drinking the solution then it means that the patient has diabetes.

A diagnosis doesn't mean your life is over. It is a starting point for managing your health better. If you are diagnosed with type 2 diabetes, your doctor will work with you to create a plan that may include changes in your diet, exercise and possibly medication to help control your blood sugar.

CHAPTER 2: Recognizing the Signs and Preventing Progression

Yes, it is possible to recognize the symptoms of prediabetes and stop it from progressing by taking effective measures like changes in lifestyle and diet. The early symptoms of diabetes act as warning sign and they must be taken seriously.

How is Prediabetes Different from Full-Blown Diabetes?
Let's clear up the difference. When you have full-blown diabetes, your body fails to produce insulin to metabolize the blood glucose. But in pre-diabetes, the body becomes insulin resistant. It is like the insulin key isn't turning the sugar lock properly. If you don't do anything about it, your body might stop making enough insulin and then you have diabetes.

The Importance of Prevention
Now, let's discuss why preventing pre-diabetes from turning into diabetes is super important.
- It is Easier to Stop in its Tracks: Pre-diabetes is like a fork in the road. You can select the path that leads to a healthier you. If you ignore it, you might end up on the diabetes road, which is more challenging.
- No Need for Medication: Most people with pre-diabetes don't need medication. You can often control it with some lifestyle changes.
- Avoid Diabetes Complications: Diabetes can bring along a bunch of problems like heart disease, eye issues and kidney troubles. Preventing pre-diabetes means avoiding these complications too.
- Healthier and Happier Life: When you prevent diabetes, you get to enjoy a better quality of life. When you have more energy, you feel good and you can do the things you love without health getting in the way.

How to Prevent Pre-Diabetes from Progressing
The good news is that you have the power to prevent pre-diabetes from turning into full-blown diabetes. Here is how:
- Eat a Healthy Diet: Select foods that are good for your blood sugar. Lots of veggies, whole grains, lean proteins and fruits (in moderation) should be on your plate. Say goodbye to sugary drinks and too much junk food.
- Stay Active: Get moving! Regular physical activity allows your body use insulin effectively. You don't have to run a marathon, just take a brisk walk, dance, or play your favorite sport.
- Lose Some Weight: Even losing a little weight can make a big difference. Shedding those extra pounds helps your body handle sugar better.
- Watch Portion Sizes: Be mindful of how much you eat. Smaller portions can help keep your blood sugar in check.
- Reduce Stress: Stress can mess with your blood sugar. Find ways to relax, whether it is through meditation, deep breathing, or hobbies you enjoy.
- Get Regular Check-Ups: Visit your doctor regularly to keep tabs on your blood sugar. They can guide you on your path to better health.
- Quit Smoking and Limit Alcohol: Smoking and too much alcohol can make blood sugar problems worse. If you smoke, try to quit and if you drink, do it in moderation.
- Sleep Well: Aim for seven to nine hours of good sleep each night. Improper sleep can mess with your blood sugar levels.

Pre-diabetes is a sign that your body needs some attention. But it's also an opportunity to take charge of your health. With some simple lifestyle changes, you can prevent it from turning into diabetes and enjoy a happier, healthier life.

CHAPTER 3: Complications and Risks Associated with Type 2 Diabetes

Yes, you can manage the symptoms and risks that are associated with Type 2 diabetes but when left unchecked this condition can lead to various healthy related complications. Before we begin to understand the ways that can help prevent the damage, it is also important to know the long-term and short-term complications so that you can take necessary steps in due time.

Short-term Complications:

Some complications of type 2 diabetes need immediate attention and you may have to consult your health expert immediately to receive the necessary medical care. So, if you experience any of the following problems, do not wait and take all the necessary steps swiftly.

- Hyperglycemia: Hyper means high and glycemia means sugar levels. In simple words this condition happens when you suffer from extremely high levels of glucose in the blood which is highly damaging to the body's organs. Extreme thirst, frequent urination and fatigue are some of the symptoms of this condition. To manage this, you need to take insulin medication.
- Hypoglycemia: It is the extremely low levels of blood sugar that cause this condition. It causes symptoms like shakiness, sweating and confusion. In this condition it is important to eat a snack or drink fruit juice to raise your blood sugar.
- Ketoacidosis: When there is not enough glucose available in the body, it breaks down fat to produce energy and ketones. In ketoacidosis, too many ketones are produced, which are highly acidic and cause serious disruption to the metabolism. Symptoms of this condition include difficulty in breathing and a fruity smell in the breath. It is crucial to get medical help right away if you experience these symptoms.

Long-term Complications:

There are several long-term complications that can develop over time if blood sugar levels are not well maintained, such as:

- Kidney Disease: Diabetes can be damaging to the kidneys, which then leads to chronic kidney disease. With regular check-ups and management of blood sugar patients can prevent kidney problems.
- Heart Disease: High sugar levels can damage blood vessels and heart muscles which can cause several cardiac diseases. By controlling your blood sugar and following a heart-healthy regime with a balanced diet and regular exercise you can reduce this risk.
- Nerve Damage: Diabetes can also cause nerve damage, which leads to symptoms like tingling or numbness in hands and feet. With blood sugar control you can prevent or slow down nerve damage.
- Eye Problems: Diabetes can affect the eyes, which leads to conditions like diabetic retinopathy. Regular eye exams are essential to catch and treat these issues early.

Monitoring and Control

In the management of type 2 diabetes, monitoring and control play a central role in ensuring a healthier and more fulfilling life. These practices are your allies in preventing complications and maintaining well-being.

How to Monitor Blood Sugar Level?

When you check your blood glucose levels on a regular basis it is like having a compass that guides you through the diabetes journey. Your healthcare team will provide guidelines on how often to test and these readings offer valuable insights into your condition. By monitoring, you can:

- Regular checks help you see how well your treatment plan is going. If your blood glucose levels are consistently high or low, it may be necessary to adjust your medications, lifestyle, or diet.
- Monitoring lets you catch and manage low or high blood sugar points before they become severe. This proactive approach can prevent immediate health risks.
- Your healthcare expert can work with you to create a personalized blood sugar plan. These plans help you maintain a stable and healthy range, reducing the risk of complications.

Diet and Physical Activity

They both are the two essential pillars of a healthy diabetes management regimen. Here is why they matter:

- Balanced Diet: When you consume a well-balanced diet, it helps regulate blood sugar levels. It allows a steady supply of nutrients while avoiding instant spikes or drops in blood sugar. A diet loaded with whole grains, veggies, lean proteins and healthy fats provides sustained energy.
- Portion Control: It is vital to monitor your portions, as even healthy foods can impact blood sugar if consumed excessively. Your dietitian can help you understand appropriate portion sizes tailored to your specific needs.
- Physical Activity: Regular exercise allows your body to use insulin more effectively and keeps blood sugar in check. It also aids in maintaining a healthy weight, reducing the risk of heart disease and improving overall well-being.

Medication Adherence

If your healthcare team suggests medication, it is crucial to consume it along with a healthy diet. Medications can help regulate blood sugar and prevent complications. Remember to:

- Follow Procedure: Always take your medications as prescribed, at the recommended times and in the right doses. If you have concerns or experience side effects, communicate with your healthcare provider.
- Go for Check-Ups: Schedule your appointments regularly with your doctor to review your medication regimen and adjust it if needed. Medications may require fine-tuning over time.

Stop Smoking

Smoking and diabetes are a dangerous combination. Smoking can cause complications and increase the risk of several other diseases. If you are a smoker, consider quitting to protect your health. Look for the help of professionals or join programs to quit smoking.

Support from Your Healthcare Team

Lastly, remember that you don't have to navigate the journey of type 2 diabetes alone. Your healthcare team, consisting of doctors, dietitians, diabetes educators and other specialists, is there to guide and support you. They have the expertise to help you make informed decisions about your health, provide valuable advice and adjust your treatment plan as your needs change.

CHAPTER 4: Managing Diabetes Through Diet

Your diet plays a crucial role in managing type 2 diabetes. In this understanding the concept of the glycemic index and knowing which foods to avoid and which to incorporate can help you stay in control.

The Glycemic Index

This Index is a scale that tells us how quickly a certain food can raise our glucose sugar. Foods with a high value of GI are quickly digested and can cause an instant blood sugar spike, while foods with a low GI are digested more slowly and result in a gradual blood sugar increase.

Foods to Avoid

- Make sure to avoid drinks with added sugars like soda, fruit juices and energy drinks. These can cause an instant blood sugar rise.
- Stay away from highly processed grains like white bread and sugary cereals. These foods have a high GI and can lead to blood sugar spikes.
- Skip eating candies, cookies and pastries. Choose healthier snacks like nuts or Greek yogurt with berries.
- While vegetables are generally healthy, some starchy ones like potatoes and corn, have a higher GI. Limit your consumption of these.

Recommended Foods

- Select whole grains like brown rice, quinoa and whole wheat bread. These have a lower GI and provide sustained energy.
- Most non-starchy fruits and vegetables have a low GI and are packed with vitamins and fiber. They are excellent choices for keeping blood sugar stable.
- Ingredients that are loaded with fiber, for instance oatmeal, lentils and broccoli, all can keep the blood sugar levels stable while helping in digestion.
- Add lean protein sources like poultry, fish, tofu and beans to your diet.
- Start consuming healthy fats like avocados, nuts and olive oil. When you incorporate healthy fats in your meals, it not only prevents high blood cholesterol levels but also keeps the heart healthy.

Perhaps, to manage type 2 diabetes through diet, we need to make smart choices, stay mindful of the glycemic index and pay attention to portion sizes.

HERE IS YOUR FREE GIFT!

- THE BEST EXERCISES FOR DIABETICS
- 30 INTERNATIONAL RECIPES FOR DIABETICS

SCAN HERE TO DOWNLOAD IT

Wholesome Oat
And Berry Bowl

🕐 **Prep:** *10 mins*   🍽 **Serves:** *2*

Directions

1. Put almond milk and oats into a microwave-safe dish and microwave on high setting for around 1 minute.
2. Take off from microwave and merge in the egg white to incorporate thoroughly.
3. Put in cinnamon and merge to incorporate thoroughly.
4. Microwave on high setting for around 2 minutes, blending after every 20 seconds.
5. Enjoy moderate hot with a topping of berries.

Ingredients

One and half C. unsweetened almond milk - One C. gluten-free quick-cooking oats - Two egg whites - Half tsp. powdered cinnamon - Quarter C. fresh strawberries - Quarter C. fresh blueberries

NUTRITIONAL VALUES : TOTAL CALORIES: 247; TOTAL CARBOHYDRATES: 36.2G; DIETARY FIBER: 7.5G; SUGARS: 3.7G; PROTEIN: 11.8G; TOTAL FAT: 5.7G; SATURATED FAT: 0.1G

Scrambled Tofu
Veggie Delight

🕐 **Prep:** *10 mins*   🍲 **Cook:** *10 mins*   🍽 **Serves:** *2*

Directions

1. Sizzle oil into a wok on burner at moderate heat.
2. Cook the bell pepper and onion for around 3-5 minutes, blending frequently.
3. Put in tomatoes and cook for around 1-2 minutes.
4. Put in tofu, turmeric, cayenne powder and salt and cook for around 6-8 minutes.
5. Enjoy right away.

Ingredients

One tbsp. olive oil - One small-sized onion, finely cut up - One small-sized bell pepper, seeded and finely cut up - Half C. cherry tomatoes, finely cut up - One and half C. firm tofu, pressed, drained and crumbled - Quarter tsp. cayenne powder - One pinch of powdered turmeric - Salt, as desired

NUTRITIONAL VALUES : TOTAL CALORIES: 234; TOTAL CARBOHYDRATES: 12.8G; DIETARY FIBER: 3.9G; SUGARS: 6G; PROTEIN: 16.9G; TOTAL FAT: 15.2G; SATURATED FAT: 2.7G

Avocado & Tomato
Whole-Wheat Toast

🕐 **Prep:** *10 mins*　　🍲 **Cook:** *16 mins*　　🍽 **Serves:** *2*

Directions

1. Put the avocado into a bowl and with a fork, mash roughly.
2. Put in the lemon juice, mint, salt and pepper and merge to incorporate thoroughly. Put it to one side.
3. Sizzle an anti-sticking frying cooking pot on burner at moderate-high heat.
4. Toast 1 bread slice for around 2 minutes from both sides.
5. Toast the remnant slices in the same manner.
6. Spread the avocado mixture over each slice.
7. Top each with tomato slices and enjoy right away.

Ingredients

One large-sized avocado, peel removed, pitted and roughly cut up - Quarter tsp. fresh lemon juice - Two tbsp. fresh mint leaves, finely cut up - Salt and powdered black pepper, as desired - Four whole-wheat bread slices - One large-sized tomato, slivered

NUTRITIONAL VALUES : TOTAL CALORIES: 300; TOTAL CARBOHYDRATES: 31.2G; DIETARY FIBER: 10.1G; SUGARS: 3.7G; PROTEIN: 8.8G; TOTAL FAT: 19.2G; SATURATED FAT: 3.5G

Almond Butter & Banana
Sandwich

🕐 **Prep:** *10 mins*　　🍲 **Cook:** *6 mins*　　🍽 **Serves:** *2*

Directions

1. Spray a large-sized anti-sticking wok with oil mist and then sizzle it on burner at moderate heat.
2. Spread the almond butter over 1 side of both bread slices.
3. Place banana slices over the buttered side of 1 slice.
4. Cover with the remnant slice and press firmly.
5. Cook the sandwiches for around 3 minutes from both sides.
6. Cut the sandwiches in half and enjoy right away.

Ingredients

Olive oil mist - Four whole-wheat bread slices, toasted - Four tsp. almond butter - One banana, peel removed and slivered

NUTRITIONAL VALUES : TOTAL CALORIES: 233; TOTAL CARBOHYDRATES: 36.7G; DIETARY FIBER: 5.2G; SUGARS: 9.4G; PROTEIN: 8.7G; TOTAL FAT: 8.9G; SATURATED FAT: 0.7G

Cinnamon Chia Seed
Pudding

🕐 **Prep:** *10 mins*   🍽 **Serves:** *3*

Directions

1. Put almond milk, chia seeds, stevia, vanilla extract and cinnamon into a large-sized bowl and merge to incorporate thoroughly.
2. Shift into your refrigerator for around 3-4 hours, blending from time to time.
3. Enjoy with the strawberry and almond slices topping.

Ingredients

Two C. unsweetened almond milk - Half C. chia seeds - Three-four drops liquid stevia - One tsp. vanilla extract - Quarter tsp. powdered cinnamon - One third C. fresh strawberries, hulled and slivered - Two tbsp. almonds, slivered

NUTRITIONAL VALUES : TOTAL CALORIES: 136; TOTAL CARBOHYDRATES: 11.6G; DIETARY FIBER: 8.2G; SUGARS: 1.1G; PROTEIN: 5.6G; TOTAL FAT: 11G; SATURATED FAT: 0.9G

Veggie-Packed
Omelette

🕐 **Prep:** *15 mins*   ▣ **Cook:** *25 mins*   🍽 **Serves:** *4*

Directions

1. For preheating: set your oven at 350ºF.
2. Lightly spray a pie dish with oil mist.
3. Put eggs, almond milk, salt and pepper into a bowl and whisk to incorporate thoroughly.
4. Put onion, bell pepper, mushrooms and tomato into a separate bowl and merge to incorporate thoroughly.
5. Put the veggie mixture into pie dish and then top it with egg mixture.
6. Sprinkle with chives.
7. Bake in your oven for around 20-25 minutes.
8. Take off the pie dish from oven and cut into 4 portions.
9. Enjoy right away.

Ingredients

Olive oil mist - Six large-sized eggs - Half C. unsweetened almond milk - Salt and powdered black pepper, as desired - Quarter C. onion, cut up - Quarter C. bell pepper, seeded and cut up - Quarter C. fresh mushrooms, slivered - Quarter C. tomato, cut up - One tbsp. fresh chive, finely cut up

NUTRITIONAL VALUES : TOTAL CALORIES: 121; TOTAL CARBOHYDRATES: 2.8G; DIETARY FIBER: 0.6G; SUGARS: 1.6G; PROTEIN: 10G; TOTAL FAT: 8G; SATURATED FAT: 2.4G

Quinoa & Fruit
Salad

🕐 **Prep:** *15 mins*   📠 **Cook:** *20 mins*   🍽 **Serves:** *4*

Directions

1. Put water, quinoa and salt into a cooking pot on burner at high heat.
2. Cook the mixture until boiling.
3. Immediately turn the heat at low.
4. Cook with the cover for around 15 minutes.
5. Shift the quinoa into a large-sized bowl.
6. Put in remnant salad ingredients and merge to incorporate.
7. For the dressing: put oil, lemon juice, salt and pepper into a separate bowl and merge to incorporate thoroughly.
8. Place dressing over quinoa mixture and merge to incorporate thoroughly.
9. Enjoy right away.

Ingredients

For the Salad:
Two C. water - One C. quinoa, rinsed - Salt, as desired - One C. fresh strawberries, slivered - One C. fresh blueberries - Two tbsp. fresh mint, cut up
For the Dressing:
Two tbsp. olive oil - Two tbsp. fresh lemon juice
Salt and powdered black pepper, as desired

NUTRITIONAL VALUES : TOTAL CALORIES: 252; TOTAL CARBOHYDRATES: 35.7G; DIETARY FIBER: 4.8G; SUGARS: 5.5G; PROTEIN: 6.7G; TOTAL FAT: 9.9G; SATURATED FAT: 1.4G

Low-Sugar
Blueberry Muffins

🕐 **Prep:** *10 mins*   📠 **Cook:** *12 mins*   🍽 **Serves:** *5*

Directions

1. For preheating: set your oven at 375ºF.
2. Spray 10 C. of a muffin tin with oil mist.
3. Put oats and remnant ingredients except for blueberries into a mixer and whirl to form a perfectly silky mixture.
4. Shift the mixture into a bowl and gently blend in blueberries.
5. Place the mixture into muffin cups.
6. Bake in your oven for around 10-12 minutes.
7. Take off the muffin tin from oven and place it onto the cooling grid for around 9-10 minutes.
8. Carefully turn the muffins onto the cooling grid to allow them to reach room temperature before enjoying.

Ingredients

Olive oil mist - Half C. rolled oats - Quarter C. almond flour - Half tsp. baking soda - Two tbsp. flaxseeds - Half tsp. powdered cinnamon - One pinch of powdered nutmeg - One egg - Quarter C. almond butter, softened - Two tbsp. banana, peel removed and slivered - Half tsp. vanilla extract - Quarter C. fresh blueberries

NUTRITIONAL VALUES : TOTAL CALORIES: 109; TOTAL CARBOHYDRATES: 9.7G; DIETARY FIBER: 2.7G; SUGARS: 1.7G; PROTEIN: 3G; TOTAL FAT: 5.8G; SATURATED FAT: 0.7G

Spinach & Mushroom
Frittata

⏱ **Prep:** *15 mins*   🍲 **Cook:** *25 mins*   🍽 **Serves:** *6*

Directions

1. For preheating: set your oven at 375°F.
2. Put almond milk, eggs, dried herbs and salt into a large-sized bowl and whisk thoroughly. Put it to one side.
3. Sizzle half of oil into an ovenproof wok on burner at moderate-high heat.
4. Cook the onion for around 3 minutes.
5. Put in mushrooms and cook for around 4-5 minutes.
6. Put in spinach and cook for around 2-3 minutes.
7. Shift the vegetable mixture into a bowl.
8. Sizzle the remnant oil into the same wok on burner at moderate-low heat.
9. Put in egg mixture and tilt the cooking pot to spread the mixture.
10. Cook for around 5 minutes.
11. Spread the vegetable mixture over cooked egg mixture.
12. Immediately, shift the wok into oven and Bake in your oven for around 5 minutes.
13. Take off the wok from oven and carefully flip the frittata.
14. Bake in your oven for around 3-4 minutes more.
15. Take off the wok of frittata from oven and put it to one side for around 5 minutes before enjoying.
16. Cut the frittata into serving portions and enjoy right away.

Ingredients

Half C. unsweetened almond milk - Twelve large-sized eggs - Half tsp. dried thyme - Half tsp. dried parsley - Salt, as desired - Two tbsp. olive oil, divided - One small-sized onion, cut up finely - One C. fresh mushrooms, slivered - One C. fresh spinach, cut up

NUTRITIONAL VALUES : TOTAL CALORIES: 195; TOTAL CARBOHYDRATES: 2.6G; DIETARY FIBER: 0.6G; SUGARS: 1.5G; PROTEIN: 13.3G; TOTAL FAT: 15G; SATURATED FAT: 3.8G

Classic Egg
Salad on Rye

🕐 **Prep:** *10 mins*   🍽 **Serves:** *2*

Directions

1. Put the eggs into a bowl and with a fork, mash roughly.
2. Put in the remnant ingredients and merge to incorporate.
3. Spread the egg mixture over each slice and enjoy right away.

Ingredients

Two hard-boiled eggs, peel removed - Two tbsp. fat-free plain Greek yogurt - Two tbsp. reduced-fat mayonnaise - One tsp. fresh chives, finely cut up - One tsp. fresh dill, finely cut up - Salt and powdered black pepper, as desired - Four rye bread slices

NUTRITIONAL VALUES : TOTAL CALORIES: 232; TOTAL CARBOHYDRATES: 25.6G; DIETARY FIBER: 6.1G; SUGARS: 3.6G; PROTEIN: 11.2G; TOTAL FAT: 9.5G; SATURATED FAT: 2.3G

Poached Eggs
With Avocado Salad

🕐 **Prep:** *10 mins*    **Cook:** *5 mins*   **Serves:** *2*

Directions

1. For the salad: put quinoa salad greens, tomatoes, avocado, lemon juice, salt and pepper into a large-sized bowl and merge to incorporate.
2. Divide the salad onto serving plates.
3. Put water into a medium-sized cooking pot on burner a moderate-high heat.
4. Cook the water until boiling and immediately turn the heat at around low.
5. Crack 2 eggs into 2 small-sized bowls.
6. With a spoon, stir the boiling water into a circular motion.
7. Carefully put both eggs into the water.
8. Cook for around 2-3 minutes.
9. With a frying ladle, shift the eggs onto each plate over salad.
10. Sprinkle each egg with salt and pepper and enjoy right away.

Ingredients

Half C. cooked quinoa - Four C. fresh salad greens - Half C. cherry tomatoes, halved - One medium-sized avocado, peel removed, pitted and slivered - One tbsp. fresh lemon juice - Salt and powdered black pepper, as desired - Two large-sized eggs

NUTRITIONAL VALUES : TOTAL CALORIES: 358; TOTAL CARBOHYDRATES: 37.2G; DIETARY FIBER: 10.7G; SUGARS: 3.8G; PROTEIN: 14.1G; TOTAL FAT: 18.4G; SATURATED FAT: 4G

Mixed Seed and Nut
Porridge

🕐 **Prep:** *15 mins* ▦ **Cook:** *40 mins* 🍽 **Serves:** *5*

Directions

1. Put the pecans, walnuts and sunflower seeds into the food mixer and whirl to form a crumbly mixture.
2. Put the nut mixture, chia seeds, coconut flakes, almond milk, spices and stevia powder into a large-sized cooking pot on burner at moderate heat.
3. Cook the mixture until boiling, blending frequently.
4. Immediately turn the heat at low.
5. Cook for around 20-30 minutes, blending frequently.
6. Take off from burner and enjoy right away.

Ingredients

Half C. pecans - Half C. walnuts - Quarter C. sunflower seeds - Quarter C. chia seeds - Quarter C. reduced-fat unsweetened coconut flakes - Four C. unsweetened almond milk - Half tsp. powdered cinnamon - Quarter tsp. powdered ginger - One tsp. stevia powder - One C. fresh blueberries

NUTRITIONAL VALUES : TOTAL CALORIES: 314; TOTAL CARBOHYDRATES: 13.8G; DIETARY FIBER: 7.5G; SUGARS: 3G; PROTEIN: 7.2G; TOTAL FAT: 19.3G; SATURATED FAT: 3.8G

Zucchini & Walnut
Bread

🕐 **Prep:** *15 mins* ▦ **Cook:** *40 mins* 🍽 **Serves:** *10*

Directions

1. For preheating: set your oven at 350ºF.
2. Lay out bakery paper into a bread mold and then spray it with oil mist lightly.
3. Put the flour, baking soda, cinnamon and salt into a bowl and merge to incorporate thoroughly.
4. Put the eggs, stevia powder and vanilla extract into a second bowl and whisk to incorporate thoroughly.
5. Put in the flour mixture and merge until just incorporated.
6. Gently blend in the grated zucchini and walnuts.
7. Put the bread mixture into the bread mold.
8. Bake in your oven for around 40 minutes.
9. Take off the bread cooking pot from oven and place it onto the cooling grid for around 9-10 minutes.
10. Carefully turn the bread onto the cooling grid to allow it to reach room temperature.
11. Cut the bread loaf into slices and enjoy right away.

Ingredients

Olive oil mist - Two C. blanched almond flour - One tsp. baking soda - One tbsp. ground cinnamon - Quarter tsp. salt - Three large-sized eggs - One and half tsp. stevia powder - One tsp. vanilla extract - Three medium-sized zucchinis, grated and squeezed - One third C. walnuts, cut up

NUTRITIONAL VALUES : TOTAL CALORIES: 194; TOTAL CARBOHYDRATES: 7.9G; DIETARY FIBER: 3.7G; SUGARS: 1.3G; PROTEIN: 8.4G; TOTAL FAT: 14.7G; SATURATED FAT: 1.4G

Berries Yogurt
Bowl

🕐 **Prep:** *10 mins*   🍽 **Serves:** *2*

Directions

1. Put the yogurt and cinnamon into a large-sized bowl and merge to incorporate thoroughly.
2. Divide the yogurt mixture in 2 serving dishes.
3. Top with berries and walnuts and enjoy right away.

Ingredients

One C. fat-free plain Greek yogurt - Quarter tsp. powdered cinnamon - Quarter C. fresh blackberries - Quarter C. fresh blueberries - Quarter C. fresh raspberries - Two tbsp. walnuts, cut up

NUTRITIONAL VALUES : TOTAL CALORIES: 144; TOTAL CARBOHYDRATES: 16.6G; DIETARY FIBER: 3.1G; SUGARS: 12G; PROTEIN: 20G; TOTAL FAT: 5.1G; SATURATED FAT: 0.4G

Mixed Berry
Smoothie with Kale

🕐 **Prep:** *10 mins*   🍽 **Serves:** *2*

Directions

1. Put kale and remnant ingredients into a high-power mixer and whirl to form a perfectly silky mixture.
2. Enjoy right away.

Ingredients

Two C. fresh kale, trimmed and cut up - One C. mixed fresh berries - Two-three drops liquid stevia - One and half C. unsweetened almond milk - Quarter C. ice cubes

NUTRITIONAL VALUES : TOTAL CALORIES: 73; TOTAL CARBOHYDRATES: 11G; DIETARY FIBER: 2.7G; SUGARS: 3.1G; PROTEIN: 2.9G; TOTAL FAT: 2.6G; SATURATED FAT: 0.3G

Pumpkin Spice
Overnight Oats

🕐 **Prep:** *10 mins*　　🍽 **Serves:** *2*

Directions

1. Put oats and remnant ingredients except for apple into a large-sized bowl and merge to incorporate.
2. Cover the bowl of oatmeal and shift into your refrigerator overnight.
3. Top with berries and enjoy right away.
4. In the morning, stir the oatmeal and enjoy with a topping of apple slices.

Ingredients

One C. gluten-free rolled oats - Three fourth C. unsweetened almond milk - One third C. sugar-free pumpkin puree - Three-four drops liquid stevia - Half tsp. vanilla extract - Quarter tsp. powdered cinnamon - Quarter tsp. powdered ginger - One pinch of powdered cloves - One pinch of salt - One apple, cored and slivere

NUTRITIONAL VALUES : TOTAL CALORIES: 111; TOTAL CARBOHYDRATES: 18.5G; DIETARY FIBER: 3.9G; SUGARS: 3G; PROTEIN: 3.6G; TOTAL FAT: 2.8G; SATURATED FAT: 0.4G

Spinach, Feta & Tomato
Scramble

🕐 **Prep:** *15 mins*　　🍳 **Cook:** *6 mins*　　🍽 **Serves:** *4*

Directions

1. Sizzle oil into a large-sized anti-sticking wok on burner at moderate-high heat.
2. Cook the tomato and spinach for around 2-3 minutes, blending frequently.
3. Put in eggs and cook for around 2 minutes, blending all the time.
4. Blend in the cheese, salt and pepper and immediately take off from pan.
5. Enjoy right away.

Ingredients

Two tbsp. olive oil - One tomato, cut up finely - One C. fresh spinach, cut up - Six eggs, whisked - Three oz. reduced-fat feta cheese, crumbled - Salt and powdered black pepper, as desired

NUTRITIONAL VALUES : TOTAL CALORIES: 236; TOTAL CARBOHYDRATES: 2.7G; DIETARY FIBER: 0.6G; SUGARS: 1.3G; PROTEIN: 13.2G; TOTAL FAT: 8.2G; SATURATED FAT: 6.2G

Eggs & Cheese
Breakfast Wrap

🕐 **Prep:** *15 mins* ▢ **Cook:** *8 mins* 🍽 **Serves:** *2*

Ingredients

Four eggs - Salt and powdered black pepper, as desired - Two tsp. olive oil - Half C. part-skim mozzarella cheese, shredded - One tomato, slivered - Two tsp. fresh basil, cut up - Two whole-wheat tortillas - Olive oil mist

Directions

1. Put the eggs, salt, pepper into small-sized bowl and whisk to incorporate.
2. Sizzle oil into wok on burner at around moderate-low heat.
3. Put in egg mixture and cook for around 2-3 minutes, blending all the time.
4. Take off the wok form burner and put it to one side.
5. Lay out the tortillas onto a plate.
6. Spread the scrambled eggs on half of each tortilla.
7. Top with basil, tomato and mozzarella cheese.
8. Carefully fold each tortilla.
9. Spray a frying cooking pot with oil mist and sizzle on burner at moderate heat.
10. Cook the tortillas for around 1-2 minutes from both sides.
11. Enjoy right away.

NUTRITIONAL VALUES : TOTAL CALORIES: 244; TOTAL CARBOHYDRATES: 12.9G; DIETARY FIBER: 1.9G; SUGARS: 1.7G; PROTEIN: 14.7G; TOTAL FAT: 15.4G; SATURATED FAT: 4.3G

Nutty Granola with Unsweetened
Almond Milk

🕐 **Prep:** *15 mins* ▢ **Cook:** *1 hr* 🍽 **Serves:** *6*

Ingredients

Two C. gluten-free old-fashioned oats - Half C. cashews, cut up - Quarter C. almonds, cut up - Half C. reduced-fat unsweetened coconut flakes - Two tsp. powdered cinnamon - Three large-sized egg whites - Two tbsp. coconut oil, melted - One tsp. vanilla extract

Directions

1. For preheating: set your oven at 225ºF.
2. Put the oats, nuts, coconut and cinnamon into a large-sized bowl and merge to incorporate.
3. Put egg whites into a bowl and whisk to form soft peaks.
4. Gently blend the whipped egg whites into oat mixture.
5. Put in coconut oil and vanilla extract and merge to incorporate.
6. Lay out bakery paper onto a baking tray.
7. Bake in your oven for around 1 hour, blending after every 20 minutes.
8. Take off the baking tray of granola from oven and put it to one side to allow it to reach room temperature.
9. Enjoy the granola with the decoration of almond milk.

NUTRITIONAL VALUES : TOTAL CALORIES: 283; TOTAL CARBOHYDRATES: 25.7G; DIETARY FIBER: 5.1G; SUGARS: 1.2G; PROTEIN: 8.8G; TOTAL FAT: 17.3G; SATURATED FAT: 7.2G

Coconut & Almond
Pancakes

🕐 **Prep:** *10 mins*　　⊡ **Cook:** *24 mins*　　🍽 **Serves:** *6*

Directions

1. Put the eggs into a large-sized bowl and gently whisk them.
2. Put in remnant ingredients and whisk to incorporate.
3. Put it to one side for around 5 minutes.
4. Spray an anti-sticking wok with oil mist and sizzle on burner at moderate heat.
5. Add desired amount of mixture and with a spoon, spread into an even layer.
6. Cook for around 1-2 minutes on each side.
7. Cook the remnant pancakes in the same manner.
8. Enjoy moderately hot.

Ingredients

Four eggs - One third C. unsweetened almond milk - Quarter C. coconut oil, melted - Two tsp. vanilla extract - One C. almond flour - Two tbsp. coconut flour - Two tbsp. Erythritol - Two tsp. baking powder - One tsp. powdered cinnamon - One pinch of salt

NUTRITIONAL VALUES : TOTAL CALORIES: 251; TOTAL CARBOHYDRATES: 7.3G; DIETARY FIBER: 3.3G; SUGARS: 0.4G; PROTEIN: 8.1G; TOTAL FAT: 21.3G; SATURATED FAT: 9.6G

Roasted Chickpeas with
Cumin and Paprika

🕐 **Prep:** *10 mins*　　📷 **Cook:** *45 mins*　　🍽 **Serves:** *12*

Directions

1. For preheating: set your oven at 400ºF.
2. Spray a large-sized baking tray with oil mist.
3. Put chickpeas onto the baking tray.
4. Roast in your oven for around 30 minutes, blending the chickpeas after every 10 minutes.
5. In the meantime, put garlic, thyme and spices into a small-sized bowl and merge to incorporate.
6. Take off the baking tray from oven.
7. Place the garlic mixture and oil over the chickpeas and merge to incorporate thoroughly.
8. Roast in your oven for around 10-15 minutes more.
9. Now, turn the oven off but leave the baking tray inside for around 9-10 minutes before enjoying.

Ingredients

Anti-sticking oil mist - Four C. cooked chickpeas - Two cloves' garlic, finely cut up - Half tsp. dried oregano - Half tsp. paprika - Quarter tsp. powdered cumin - Sea salt, as desired - One tbsp. olive oil

NUTRITIONAL VALUES : TOTAL CALORIES: 92; TOTAL CARBOHYDRATES: 15G; DIETARY FIBER: 0.1G; SUGARS: 4G; PROTEIN: 4.1G; TOTAL FAT: 1.9G; SATURATED FAT: 0.2G

Crunchy Veggie Sticks
With Hummus Dip

🕐 **Prep:** *15 mins*　　🍽 **Serves:** *4*

Directions

1. Put the chickpeas, tahini, lemon juice, clove garlic, oil, cumin, salt and pepper into the food mixer and whirl to form a perfectly silky mixture.
2. Shift the hummus into a small-sized bowl and enjoy alongside the veggie sticks.

Ingredients

Two large-sized carrots, peel removed and cut into sticks - Two medium-sized cucumbers, cut into sticks -Two medium-sized cucumbers, cut into sticks - Two bell peppers (multi-colored), seeded and cut into sticks - One celery stalk, cut into sticks - Fifteen oz. canned chickpeas, drained - Two tbsp. tahini - Two tbsp. lemon juice - One clove garlic, finely cut up - Two tbsp. olive oil - Quarter tsp. powdered cumin - Quarter tsp. paprika - Salt and powdered black pepper, as desired

NUTRITIONAL VALUES : TOTAL CALORIES: 284; TOTAL CARBOHYDRATES: 38G; DIETARY FIBER: 8.2G; SUGARS: 6G; PROTEIN: 8.5G; TOTAL FAT: 12.6G; SATURATED FAT: 1.8G

Almond-Stuffed
Medjool Dates

🕐 **Prep:** *10 mins*   🍽 **Serves:** *2*

Directions

1. Stuff each date with an almond.
2. Enjoy right away.

Ingredients

Six Medjool dates, pitted
Six salted whole almonds

Unsweetened
Cocoa-Dusted Almonds

🕐 **Prep:** *10 mins*   🍲 **Cook:** *15 mins*   🍽 **Serves:** *4*

Directions

1. For preheating: set your oven at 350ºF.
2. Put vanilla extract and honey into a medium-sized bowl and merge to incorporate.
3. Put in almonds and coat with mixture thoroughly.
4. Dust almonds with cocoa powder and salt.
5. Lay out the coated almonds onto a baking tray.
6. Roast in your oven for around 15 minutes.
7. Take off the baking tray from oven and put it to one side for around 9-10 minutes before enjoying.

Ingredients

One tbsp. honey - Quarter tsp. vanilla extract -
One C. all natural almonds - Quarter tsp. sea salt
- One tbsp. unsweetened cocoa powder

Spicy Edamame
With Garlic and Chili

🕐 **Prep:** *10 mins* 📱 **Cook:** *20 mins* 🍽 **Serves:** *4*

Directions

1. For preheating: set your oven at 450ºF.
2. Spray a large-sized baking tray with oil mist.
3. In a bowl, put edamame and remnant ingredients and merge to incorporate.
4. Place the edamame onto the baking tray and spread in an even layer.
5. Roast for around 15-20 minutes, blending once halfway through.
6. Take off from oven and let the edamame cool thoroughly before enjoying.

Ingredients

Anti-sticking oil mist - Two C. frozen shelled edamame, thawed - One clove garlic, finely cut up - Two tsp. olive oil - One tsp. red chili powder - Half tsp. powdered cumin - One tsp. sea salt

NUTRITIONAL VALUES : TOTAL CALORIES: 208; TOTAL CARBOHYDRATES: 14.1G; DIETARY FIBER: 5.4G; SUGARS: 0G; PROTEIN: 16.6G; TOTAL FAT: 11G; SATURATED FAT: 1.3G

Cucumber and Tuna
Salad Cups

🕐 **Prep:** *15 mins* 🍽 **Serves:** *2*

Directions

1. Cut the cucumber into 2-3-inch-long sections.
2. With a small-sized spoon, hollow out each section to form a cup.
3. With paper towels, gently pat the inside of each cucumber cup.
4. In a medium-sized bowl, put the tuna, mayonnaise, celery, salt and pepper and merge to incorporate.
5. Spoon the tuna mixture into each cucumber C. and enjoy right away.

Ingredients

Two medium-sized English cucumbers - Ten oz. water-packed canned tuna, drained - Six tbsp. mayonnaise - Half C. diced celery - Two tbsp. red onion, finely cut up - Two tsp. fresh parsley, finely cut up - Salt and powdered black pepper, as desired - Two tsp. Everything Bagel Seasoning

NUTRITIONAL VALUES : TOTAL CALORIES: 280; TOTAL CARBOHYDRATES: 16G; DIETARY FIBER: 2G; SUGARS: 7G; PROTEIN: 29G; TOTAL FAT: 6G; SATURATED FAT: 2G

Savory Roasted
Pumpkin Seeds

🕐 **Prep:** *10 mins*   🍲 **Cook:** *20 mins*   🍽 **Serves:** *4*

Directions

1. For preheating: set your oven at 350°F.
2. Put pumpkin seeds and remnant ingredients except for lemon juice to a bowl and merge to incorporate.
3. Shift the pumpkin seeds mixture onto a baking tray.
4. Roast for around 20 minutes, flipping from time to time.
5. Take off from oven and put to one side to allow it to reach room temperature before enjoying.
6. Drizzle with the lemon juice and enjoy right away.

Ingredients

One C. pumpkin seeds, washed and dried - Two tsp. garam masala powder - One third tsp. red chili powder - Quarter tsp. powdered turmeric - Sea salt, as desired - Three tbsp. coconut oil, meted - Half tbsp. fresh lemon juice

NUTRITIONAL VALUES : TOTAL CALORIES: 276; TOTAL CARBOHYDRATES: 6.4G; DIETARY FIBER: 1.5G; SUGARS: 0.4G; PROTEIN: 8.6G; TOTAL FAT: 26.1G; SATURATED FAT: 11.8G

Nutty No-Bake
Energy Bites

🕐 **Prep:** *15 mins*   🍽 **Serves:** *8*

Directions

1. In a bowl, place the dates and top with hot water. Put to one side for around 5 minutes.
2. Drain the dates well.
3. In the food mixer, put the dates, peanut butter and salt and whirl to form a perfectly silky mixture.
4. Put in remnant ingredients and whirl until just incorporated.
5. Make small-sized balls from the mixture.
6. Lay out the balls onto a bakery paper-lined baking tray.
7. Shift into your refrigerator to set for around 2 hours before enjoying.

Ingredients

Nine Medjool dates, pitted - Two tbsp. natural peanut butter - One pinch of salt - Half C. roasted unsalted peanuts - One third C. gluten-free oats - Half C. unsweetened coconut, shredded - Two tbsp. cacao powder - One scoop unsweetened vanilla protein powder

NUTRITIONAL VALUES : TOTAL CALORIES: 202; TOTAL CARBOHYDRATES: 26.2G; DIETARY FIBER: 4.1G; SUGARS: 36.1G; PROTEIN: 8.2G; TOTAL FAT: 9.7G; SATURATED FAT: 1.9G

Zesty Lemon & Herb
Greek Yogurt Dip

🕐 **Prep:** *10 mins*   🍽 **Serves:** *12*

Directions

1. In a medium-sized bowl, yogurt and remnant ingredients and merge to incorporate.
2. Cover the bowl of dip and shift into your refrigerator for around 30 minutes.

Ingredients

One and half C. fat-free plain yogurt - One and half tbsp. lemon juice - One tsp. lemon zest, grated - One clove garlic, grated - One tsp. powdered cumin - Half tsp. sea salt

NUTRITIONAL VALUES : TOTAL CALORIES: 20; TOTAL CARBOHYDRATES: 2G; DIETARY FIBER: 1G; SUGARS: 1G; PROTEIN: 1G; TOTAL FAT: 1G; SATURATED FAT: 1G

Oven-Baked
Sweet Potato Chips

🕐 **Prep:** *15 mins*   📟 **Cook:** *25 mins*   🍽 **Serves:** *8*

Directions

1. For preheating: set your oven at 300ºF.
2. Line 2-3 large-sized baking trays with bakery paper.
3. Put the sweet potato rounds and oil into a large-sized bowl and merge to incorporate.
4. Lay out the sweet potato rounds onto the baking trays.
5. Sprinkle with salt.
6. Bake in your oven for around 20-25 minutes.
7. Take off the baking trays from oven and put to one side for around 5-6 minutes before enjoying.

Ingredients

One and half lb. sweet potatoes, peel removed and cut into paper-thin rounds - One third C. olive oil - Salt, as desired

NUTRITIONAL VALUES : TOTAL CALORIES: 152; TOTAL CARBOHYDRATES: 17G; DIETARY FIBER: 2G; SUGARS: 3G; PROTEIN: 20G; TOTAL FAT: 9G; SATURATED FAT: 1G

Cheesy
Kale Chips

🕐 **Prep:** *10 mins*　　📠 **Cook:** *15 mins*　　🍽 **Serves:** *6*

Directions

1. For preheating: set your oven at 350°F.
2. Line 2 baking trays with bakery paper.
3. In a large-sized bowl, put kale pieces, oil and salt and merge to incorporate.
4. Place the kale pieces onto the baking trays.
5. Bake in your oven for around 9-10 minutes.
6. After 10 minutes of cooking sprinkle the kale pieces with Parmesan cheese.
7. Bake in your oven for around 5 minutes.
8. Take off the baking trays from oven and put to one side to cool before enjoying.

Ingredients

One large-sized bunch flat-leaf kale, tough ribs removed and torn - Two-three tbsp. olive oil - Salt, as desired - Half C. Parmesan cheese, grated

NUTRITIONAL VALUES : TOTAL CALORIES: 61; TOTAL CARBOHYDRATES: 4G; DIETARY FIBER: 0.1G; SUGARS: 1.2G; PROTEIN: 3G; TOTAL FAT: 3G; SATURATED FAT: 1G

Avocado and Egg
Salad Lettuce Wraps

🕐 **Prep:** *15 mins*　　🍽 **Serves:** *4*

Directions

1. In a bowl, put eggs and remnant ingredients except for lettuce and merge to incorporate.
2. Lay out the lettuce leaves onto serving plates.
3. Top each with egg mixture and enjoy right away.

Ingredients

Four boiled eggs, peel removed and cut up - One medium-sized avocado, peel removed, pitted and cut up - Two tsp. lemon juice - Three tbsp. mayonnaise - Two tbsp. fresh chives, finely cut up Half tsp. salt - Quarter tsp. powdered black pepper - Eight lettuce leaves

NUTRITIONAL VALUES : TOTAL CALORIES: 65; TOTAL CARBOHYDRATES: 0G; DIETARY FIBER: G; SUGARS: 3G; PROTEIN: 20G; TOTAL FAT: 15G; SATURATED FAT: 5G

Peanut Butter
Celery Sticks

🕐 **Prep:** *10 mins*   🛎 **Serves:** *4*

Directions

1. Cut the celery into 4-inch lengths.
2. Spread peanut butter over each celery stalk piece and enjoy right away.

Ingredients

Four celery stalks
One C. peanut butter

NUTRITIONAL VALUES : TOTAL CALORIES: 191; TOTAL CARBOHYDRATES: 6.6G; DIETARY FIBER: 2.1G; SUGARS: 3.1G; PROTEIN: 8.1G; TOTAL FAT: 16.2G; SATURATED FAT: 3.4G

Nuts & Dried
Cranberry Mix

🕐 **Prep:** *10 mins*   📟 **Cook:** *51 mins*   🛎 **Serves:** *15*

Directions

1. For preheating: set your oven at 350ºF.
2. Line two rimmed baking trays with bakery paper and then spray with oil mist.
3. In a bowl, put nuts and merge to incorporate.
4. Place the nut mixture onto the baking trays.
5. Bake in your oven for around 6 minutes.
6. Take off the nuts from oven and let them cool.
7. Now, set your oven at 225ºF.
8. Put the cooled nuts and remnant ingredients into a large-sized bowl and merge to incorporate.
9. Bake in your oven for around 45 minutes, blending after every 15 minutes.
10. Take off the nut mixture from oven and let them cool.

Ingredients

Anti-sticking oil mist - One C. unsalted cashews - One C. raw unsalted almonds - Half C. raw unsalted pecans - Half C. raw unsalted pistachios, shelled - Half C. unsweetened dried cranberries - Quarter C. Erythritol - One egg white - One tsp. vanilla extract - One tsp. powdered cinnamon - Quarter tsp. salt

---

NUTRITIONAL VALUES : TOTAL CALORIES: 160; TOTAL CARBOHYDRATES: 8G; DIETARY FIBER: 3G; SUGARS: 2G; PROTEIN: 5G; TOTAL FAT: 13G; SATURATED FAT: 1.6G

Pumpkin Seed
Clusters

🕐 **Prep:** *10 mins*　　📷 **Cook:** *8 mins*　　🍽 **Serves:** *6*

Directions

1. For preheating: set your oven at 350ºF.
2. Lay out bakery paper onto a large-sized, rimmed baking tray.
3. In a large-sized bowl, put the coconut chips and remnant ingredients and merge to incorporate.
4. With a small-sized spoon, place the mixture onto baking tray about 1-inch apart.
5. Bake in your oven for round 7-8 minutes.
6. Take off the keto coconut clusters from oven and let the clusters cool thoroughly before enjoying

Ingredients

One and half C. Unsweetened coconut chips - One third C. pumpkin seeds - One third C. sunflower seeds - One tbsp. chia seed - Two tbsp. Monk Fruit sweetener - Quarter C. honey - One tbsp. coconut oil, melted - Quarter tsp. Sea salt

NUTRITIONAL VALUES : TOTAL CALORIES: 235; TOTAL CARBOHYDRATES: 12.1G; DIETARY FIBER: 8.2G; SUGARS: 2.6G; PROTEIN: 4.3G; TOTAL FAT: 21.9G; SATURATED FAT: 5.9G

Cherry Tomato & Mozzarella
Skewers

🕐 **Prep:** *15 mins*　　🍽 **Serves:** *6*

Directions

1. In a bowl, add mozzarella balls, garlic, oil and Italian seasoning and merge to incorporate.
2. Shift into your refrigerator to marinate for around 30 minutes.
3. Thread tomatoes, basil and mozzarella balls onto skewers.
4. Drizzle with a little marinade and sprinkle with salt and pepper.
5. Enjoy right away.

Ingredients

Twelve mozzarella balls - One clove garlic, minced - Quarter C. olive oil - Half tsp. Italian seasoning - Salt and powdered black pepper, as desired - 24 cherry tomatoes - 24 small-sized basil leaves

NUTRITIONAL VALUES : TOTAL CALORIES: 91; TOTAL CARBOHYDRATES: 3G; DIETARY FIBER: 1G; SUGARS: 1G; PROTEIN: 5G; TOTAL FAT: 7G; SATURATED FAT: 2G

Lightly Salted
Air-Popped Popcorn

🕐 **Prep:** *10 mins*　　🍲 **Cook:** *5 mins*　　🍽 **Serves:** *3*

Directions

1. In a cooking pot, sizzle coconut oil on burner at moderate-high heat.
2. Put in popping corn and cover the cooking pot tightly.
3. Cook for around 1-2 minutes or until corn kernels start to pop, shaking the cooking pot from time to time.
4. Take off the cooking pot from burner and shift into a large-sized heatproof bowl.
5. Add salt and merge thoroughly.
6. Enjoy right away

Ingredients

Two tbsp. coconut oil
Three quarters C. popping corn
Quarter tsp. salt

NUTRITIONAL VALUES : TOTAL CALORIES: 112; TOTAL CARBOHYDRATES: 7.4G; DIETARY FIBER: 1.2G; SUGARS: 1.3G; PROTEIN: 1.3G; TOTAL FAT: 9.5G; SATURATED FAT: 7.9G

Spiced Guacamole
With Bell Pepper Dippers

🕐 **Prep:** *10 mins*　　🍽 **Serves:** *4*

Directions

1. In a large-sized bowl, put avocado and mash it thoroughly with a fork.
2. Put in remnant ingredients and gently blend to incorporate.
3. Enjoy right away.

Ingredients

Two medium-sized ripe avocados, peel removed, pitted and cut up - One small-sized red onion, cut up - One clove garlic, finely cut up - One Serrano pepper, seeded and cut up - One tomato, seeded and cut up - Two tbsp. fresh cilantro leaves, cut up - One tbsp. fresh lime juice - Salt, as desired

NUTRITIONAL VALUES : TOTAL CALORIES: 217; TOTAL CARBOHYDRATES: 11.3G; DIETARY FIBER: 7.4G; SUGARS: 1.7G; PROTEIN: 2.3G; TOTAL FAT: 19.7G; SATURATED FAT: 54.1G

Fresh Fruit Salad
With a Hint of Mint

🕐 **Prep:** *15 mins*　　🍽 **Serves:** *8*

Directions

1. In a large-sized salad bowl, put watermelon and remnant ingredients and gently toss to blend.
2. Enjoy right away.

Ingredients

Two and half lb. seedless watermelon, cubed - Two C. fresh strawberries, hulled and slivered - Two C. fresh blueberries - One C. fresh raspberries - One tbsp. fresh ginger root, grated - Four tbsp. fresh mint leaves, cut up - Two tbsp. honey - Quarter C. fresh lime juice

NUTRITIONAL VALUES : TOTAL CALORIES: 101; TOTAL CARBOHYDRATES: 25.3G; DIETARY FIBER: 3.4G; SUGARS: 19.1G; PROTEIN: 1.7G; TOTAL FAT: 0.6G; SATURATED FAT: 0G

Jicama, Carrot
And Apple Salad

🕐 **Prep:** *15 mins*　　🍽 **Serves:** *8*

Directions

1. For the dressing: in a mixer, put ginger and remnant ingredients and pulse to blend thoroughly.
2. In another large-sized salad bowl, blend together salad ingredients.
3. Pour dressing over salad and merge to incorporate.
4. Enjoy right away.

Ingredients

For the Dressing:
One tbsp. fresh ginger, cut up - Two tbsp. coconut cream - Two tbsp. fresh lime juice - Two tbsp. olive oil - One tsp. stevia powder
For the Salad:
One C. carrot, peel removed and julienned - One C. jicama, julienned - One C. apple, cored and julienned - Two scallions, cut up - Quarter C. fresh cilantro, cut up

NUTRITIONAL VALUES : TOTAL CALORIES: 119; TOTAL CARBOHYDRATES: 14.6G; DIETARY FIBER: 3.9G; SUGARS: 7.9G; PROTEIN: 0.9G; TOTAL FAT: 7.2G; SATURATED FAT: 1G

Grilled Chicken
Salad with Lettuce

🕐 **Prep:** *15 mins*   🍲 **Cook:** *20 mins*   🍽 **Serves:** *4*

Directions

1. For the chicken: put chicken breasts and remnant ingredients into a large-sized Ziploc bag and seal it.
2. Shake the bag to coat the chicken with marinade well.
3. Shift into your refrigerator to marinate for around 20 minutes to 1 hour.
4. For preheating: set your grill to moderate-high heat.
5. Spray the grill grate with oil mist.
6. Lay out the chicken breasts onto the grill.
7. Grill for around 9-10 minutes from both sides.
8. Take off the chicken breasts from grill and shift onto a chopping block for around 5-6 minutes.
9. In the meantime, for the salad: put lettuce and remnant ingredients into a bowl and merge to incorporate.
10. Cut each chicken breast into slices.
11. Place the salad onto a serving platter and top with chicken slices.
12. Enjoy right away.

Ingredients

For the Chicken:
Three (five-oz.) boneless chicken breasts - One-inch piece fresh ginger, finely cut up - Two cloves' garlic, finely cut up - One tsp. sesame seeds - Three tbsp. olive oil - Two tbsp. fresh lime juice - Salt and powdered black pepper, as desired - Anti-sticking oil mist

For the Salad:
Four C. lettuce, torn - One C. cherry tomatoes, halved - Quarter C. onion, slivered - Two tbsp. olive oil - Two tbsp. lemon juice - Salt and powdered black pepper, as desired

NUTRITIONAL VALUES : TOTAL CALORIES: 255; TOTAL CARBOHYDRATES: 4.1G; DIETARY FIBER: 1G; SUGARS: 1.9G; PROTEIN: 25.5G; TOTAL FAT: 15.7G; SATURATED FAT: 2.1G

Quinoa & Black Bean
Bowl with Lime Dressing

🕐 **Prep:** *15 mins*   ▣ **Cook:** *30 mins*   🍽 **Serves:** *6*

Directions

1. Put broth into a cooking pot on burner at high heat.
2. Cook the broth until boiling.
3. Blend in quinoa and salt and cook the mixture until boiling.
4. Immediately turn the heat at low.
5. Cook with the cover for around 15-20 minutes.
6. Take off the cooking pot of quinoa from burner and put it to one side with the cover for around 5-10 minutes.
7. Take of the cover and fluff the quinoa with a fork.
8. Put the cooked quinoa and remnant ingredients into a large-sized salad bowl and gently toss to incorporate.
9. Enjoy right away

Ingredients

One- and three-quarter C. vegetable broth - One C. quinoa, rinsed - Sea salt, as desired - One and half C. cooked black beans - Two medium-sized bell peppers, seeded and cut up - Two tomatoes, cut up - Quarter C. fresh cilantro, cut up - Two tbsp. olive oil

NUTRITIONAL VALUES : TOTAL CALORIES: 232; TOTAL CARBOHYDRATES: 33.3G; DIETARY FIBER: 6.8G; SUGARS: 3.3G; PROTEIN: 10G; TOTAL FAT: 7.2G; SATURATED FAT: 1.1G

Tomato & Basil
Whole Wheat Pasta Salad

🕐 **Prep:** *15 mins*   ▣ **Cook:** *10 mins*   🍽 **Serves:** *4*

Directions

1. For the salad: cook the pasta into a large-sized cooking pot of boiling water for around 8-10 minutes.
2. Drain the pasta and then rinse it thoroughly.
3. Put pasta and remnant ingredients into a large-sized salad bowl and merge to incorporate.
4. For the dressing: put oil and remnant ingredients into a small-sized bowl and whisk to incorporate thoroughly.
5. Place the dressing over salad and merge to incorporate.
6. Shift into your refrigerator to chill thoroughly before enjoying.

Ingredients

For the Salad:
Half C. uncooked whole-wheat pasta - Three plum tomatoes, cut up - One C. black olives, pitted and slivered - Six C. fresh spinach, roughly cut up - Three scallions, cut up - Half C. reduced-fat feta cheese, crumbled - One tbsp. caper, drained
For the Dressing:
One third C. olive oil - Four tsp. fresh lemon juice - One tbsp. fresh parsley, finely cut up - Two tsp. fresh lemon zest, grated - Salt and powdered black pepper, as desired

NUTRITIONAL VALUES : TOTAL CALORIES: 215; TOTAL CARBOHYDRATES: 23.6G; DIETARY FIBER: 3.3G; SUGARS: 5.2G; PROTEIN: 5G; TOTAL FAT: 12.1G; SATURATED FAT: 2.4G

Seared
Tuna with Greens

🕐 **Prep:** *10* mins   🍲 **Cook:** *2* mins   🍽 **Serves:** *2*

Directions

1. Sprinkle the tuna steaks with salt and pepper.
2. Put the sesame seeds onto a shallow plate.
3. Gently press tuna steaks into seeds to coat.
4. In a medium-sized wok, sizzle oil on burner at moderate-high heat and sear the tuna for around 1 minute from both sides or until desired doneness.
5. Shift the tuna steaks onto a chopping block.
6. Cut each tuna steak into desired sized slices and enjoy right away.

Ingredients

Two (four-oz.) ahi tuna steaks
Salt and powdered black pepper, as desired
Four tbsp. sesame seeds
One tbsp. olive oil

NUTRITIONAL VALUES : TOTAL CALORIES: 378; TOTAL CARBOHYDRATES: 56G; DIETARY FIBER: 2.8G; SUGARS: 3.7G; PROTEIN: 37.8G; TOTAL FAT: 23.1G; SATURATED FAT: 4.1G

Chickpea & Feta
Salad with Olive Dressing

🕐 **Prep:** *15* mins   🍽 **Serves:** *8*

Directions

1. For the dressing: in a bowl, put the oil, vinegar, garlic, dried herbs, salt and pepper and whisk to incorporate thoroughly.
2. In a large-sized serving dish, put the chickpeas, tomato, onion and feta cheese and merge thoroughly.
3. Place the dressing over salad and merge to incorporate.
4. Decorate with basil and enjoy right away.

Ingredients

Two tbsp. olive oil - One tbsp. balsamic vinegar - Two cloves' garlic, pressed - Half tsp. dried thyme - Half tsp. dried basil - Powdered black pepper, as desired - One (fifteen-oz.) can chickpeas, drained - One C. cherry tomatoes, halved - Half C. onion, slivered - Half C. feta cheese, crumbled - Three tbsp. fresh basil, slivered thinly

NUTRITIONAL VALUES : TOTAL CALORIES: 350; TOTAL CARBOHYDRATES: 30G; DIETARY FIBER: 3G; SUGARS: 3G; PROTEIN: 20G; TOTAL FAT: 15G; SATURATED FAT: 5G

Mediterranean Lentil
Soup with Lemon Zest

🕐 **Prep:** *15 mins*   🍲 **Cook:** *45 mins*   🍽 **Serves:** *4*

Directions

1. Sizzle the oil into a large-sized cooking pot on burner at moderate heat.
2. Cook the carrots, onion, garlic and ginger for around 3-5 minutes.
3. Put in sweet potatoes and cook for around 3-4 minutes, blending from time to time.
4. Blend in the curry powder and cook for around 2 minutes.
5. Put in lentils and broth and merge to incorporate.
6. Immediately turn the heat at medium-high.
7. Cook the mixture until boiling.
8. Immediately turn the heat at low.
9. Cook for around 20-25 minutes.
10. Blend in the kale and cook for around 3-5 minutes.
11. Blend in the lemon juice and take off from burner.
12. Enjoy right away.

Ingredients

One tbsp. coconut oil - Two medium-sized carrots, peel removed and cut up - One C. white onion, cut up - Four cloves garlic, finely cut up - One tsp. fresh ginger, finely cut up - Salt and powdered black pepper, as desired - Three C. sweet potatoes, peel removed and cubed - One and half tbsp. curry powder - Five-six C. vegetable broth One C. green lentils, rinsed and drained - Four C. fresh baby spinach - Two tbsp. fresh lemon juice

NUTRITIONAL VALUES : TOTAL CALORIES: 455; TOTAL CARBOHYDRATES: 89.6G; DIETARY FIBER: 22.5G; SUGARS: 14.6G; PROTEIN: 17.2G; TOTAL FAT: 4.5G; SATURATED FAT: 1.1G

Broccoli & Cauliflower
Salad with Mustard Vinaigrette

🕐 **Prep:** *15 mins*   🍽 **Serves:** *4*

Directions

1. Soak the onions into a bowl of ice water for around 9-10 minutes.
2. Drain the onions thoroughly.
3. In a large-sized salad bowl, put onion, broccoli, cauliflower and tomatoes and merge.
4. For the dressing: in a small-sized bowl, put remnant ingredients and whisk to incorporate.
5. Place the dressing over salad and merge to incorporate.
6. Decorate with basil and enjoy right away.

Ingredients

Quarter red onion, thinly slivered - One and half C. broccoli, cut into small-sized florets - One and half C. cauliflower, cut into small-sized florets - One C. heirloom tomatoes, halved - One tbsp. balsamic vinegar - One tsp. Dijon mustard - Two tbsp. olive oil - Quarter C. mayonnaise - Half tsp. Old Bay seasoning - Salt and powdered black pepper

NUTRITIONAL VALUES : TOTAL CALORIES: 151; TOTAL CARBOHYDRATES: 10.3G; DIETARY FIBER: 2.6G; SUGARS: 3.9G; PROTEIN: 2.4G; TOTAL FAT: 12.2G; SATURATED FAT: 1.7G

Roast Beef & Arugula
Sandwich

🕐 **Prep:** *15 mins*   🍽 **Serves:** *2*

Directions

1. Spread mayonnaise over 2 bread slices.
2. Place tomato, beef and arugula on top of mayonnaise.
3. Cover with remnant bread slices and enjoy right away.

Ingredients

Two tbsp. reduced-fat mayonnaise - Four whole-wheat bread slices - One tomato, cut into slices - Four oz. lean roast beef, thinly slivered - One C. arugula

---

NUTRITIONAL VALUES : TOTAL CALORIES: 254; TOTAL CARBOHYDRATES: 25G; DIETARY FIBER: 5.7G; SUGARS: 2.3G; PROTEIN: 23.2G; TOTAL FAT: 9.6G; SATURATED FAT: 2.1G

Hearty Vegetable
& Barley Soup

🕐 **Prep:** *15 mins*   📟 **Cook:** *40 mins*   🍽 **Serves:** *4*

Directions

1. In a large-sized soup pan, sizzle oil on burner at moderate heat.
2. Cook the onion, celery and carrot for around 4-5 minutes.
3. Put in garlic and rosemary and cook for around 1 minute.
4. Put in tomatoes and cook for 3-4 minutes, crushing with the back of a spoon.
5. Put in barley and broth and merge.
6. Cook the mixture until boiling.
7. Immediately turn the heat at low.
8. Cook with the cover for around 25-30 minutes.
9. Blend in the lemon juice and take off from burner.
10. Decorate with parsley and enjoy right away

Ingredients

One tbsp. olive oil - One white onion, cut up - Two celery stalks, cut up - One large-sized carrot, peel removed and cut up - Two tbsp. fresh rosemary, cut up - Two cloves garlic, finely cut up - Four C. fresh tomatoes, cut up - Four C. vegetable broth - One and half C. pearl barley - Two tbsp. fresh lemon juice Four tbsp. fresh parsley leaves, cut up

---

NUTRITIONAL VALUES : TOTAL CALORIES: 260; TOTAL CARBOHYDRATES: 42G; DIETARY FIBER: 10.8G; SUGARS: 6.5G; PROTEIN: 11.5G; TOTAL FAT: 5.2G; SATURATED FAT: 0.9G

Turkey & Avocado
Spinach Wrap

🕐 **Prep:** *15 mins*   🍽 **Serves:** *4*

Directions

1. In a small-sized bowl, put the avocado and yogurt and with a fork, mash to incorporate.
2. Spread avocado mixture over each tortilla.
3. Top each tortilla with turkey, sunflower seeds, tomato and lettuce.
4. Roll each tortilla and enjoy right away.

Ingredients

Half avocado, peel removed, pitted and mashed - Two tbsp. fat-free plain Greek yogurt - Four large-sized whole-wheat tortillas - Twelve oz. cooked turkey, slivered - Four tsp. sunflower seeds - One tomato, slivered - One C. lettuce, shredded

NUTRITIONAL VALUES : TOTAL CALORIES: 250; TOTAL CARBOHYDRATES: 23G; DIETARY FIBER: 15G; SUGARS: 3G; PROTEIN: 33G; TOTAL FAT: 9G; SATURATED FAT: 1.1G

Spiced Turkey & Vegetable
Stuffed Peppers

🕐 **Prep:** *15 mins*   📟 **Cook:** *20 mins*   🍽 **Serves:** *6*

Directions

1. Sizzle the coconut oil into a wok on burner at moderate-high heat.
2. Cook the garlic for around 30 seconds.
3. Put in beef and cook for around 5 minutes.
4. Put in mushrooms and onion and merge.
5. Cook for around 5-6 minutes.
6. Blend in salt and pepper and cook for around 30 seconds.
7. Take off from burner and merge in tomato puree.
8. In the meantime, in a microwave-safe dish, lay out the bell peppers, cut-side down.
9. Pour the water in baking pan.
10. With a cling wrap, cover the baking pan and microwave on high for around 4-5 minutes.
11. Take off from microwave and uncover the baking pan.
12. Drain the water thoroughly.
13. In the baking pan, lay out the bell peppers, cut-side up.
14. Stuff each bell pepper half with cooked beef mixture and then top with cheese.
15. Microwave on High for around 2-3 minutes.
16. Enjoy moderately hot.

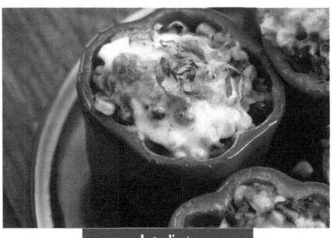

Ingredients

Two tsp. coconut oil - One lb. lean ground beef - One clove garlic, finely cut up - One C. white mushrooms, cut up - One C. yellow onion, cut up - Salt and powdered black pepper, as desired - Half C. tomato puree - Three large-sized green bell peppers, halved lengthwise and cored - One C. water - Four oz. reduced-fat cheddar cheese, shredded

NUTRITIONAL VALUES : TOTAL CALORIES: 258; TOTAL CARBOHYDRATES: 8G; DIETARY FIBER: 2.3G; SUGARS: 4.1G; PROTEIN: 21.8G; TOTAL FAT: 15.4G; SATURATED FAT: 8.4G

Spinach & Goat Cheese
Stuffed Chicken Breast

🕐 **Prep:** *15 mins*   📷 **Cook:** *30 mins*   🍽 **Serves:** *4*

Directions

1. For preheating: set your oven at 400ºF.
2. Place 1 chicken breasts onto a smooth surface.
3. Hold a knife parallel to work surface, slice the chicken breast horizontally, without cutting all the way through.
4. Lay out the chicken breasts into a baking pan.
5. Put the spinach, goat cheese, basil, salt, garlic powder and pepper into a medium-sized bowl and merge thoroughly.
6. Stuff each chicken breast with cheese mixture.
7. Bake in your oven for around 25-30 minutes.
8. Enjoy right away.

Ingredients

Four chicken breasts, pounded - Ten oz. frozen cut up spinach, thawed and drained - Eight oz. soft goat cheese - Quarter C. fresh basil, cut up - Half tsp. salt - Half tsp. garlic powder - Quarter tsp. powdered black pepper

NUTRITIONAL VALUES : TOTAL CALORIES: 430; TOTAL CARBOHYDRATES: 30G; DIETARY FIBER: 2G; SUGARS: 1G; PROTEIN: 61G; TOTAL FAT: 1G; SATURATED FAT: 10G

Balsamic Glazed
Grilled Portobello Mushrooms

🕐 **Prep:** *10 mins*   📷 **Cook:** *8 mins*   🍽 **Serves:** *6*

Directions

1. Place the mushrooms into a baking pan.
2. In a bowl, put garlic, oil, vinegar, salt and pepper and merge to incorporate.
3. Pour the balsamic sauce over mushrooms and shift into your refrigerator to marinate for 1-2 hours.
4. For preheating: set your grill to moderate heat.
5. Lay out the mushrooms onto the grill.
6. Cook for around 3-4 minutes from both sides.
7. Enjoy with a decoration of parsley.

Ingredients

Six Portobello mushrooms, stems removed
Two cloves garlic, finely cut up
Quarter C. olive oil
Quarter C. balsamic vinegar
Salt and powdered black pepper, as desired
Two tbsp. fresh parsley, cut up

NUTRITIONAL VALUES : TOTAL CALORIES: 154; TOTAL CARBOHYDRATES: 6G; DIETARY FIBER: 1G; SUGARS: 1G; PROTEIN: 2G; TOTAL FAT: 14G; SATURATED FAT: 2G

Classic Caesar
Salad with Grilled Shrimp

🕐 **Prep:** *20 mins*   📷 **Cook:** *6 mins*   🍽 **Serves:** *6*

Directions

1. For the shrimp: put the shrimp, oil, garlic, lemon zest, salt and pepper into a large-sized bowl and merge to incorporate.
2. Put the bowl aside at room temperature for around 20 minutes.
3. For preheating: set your grill to moderate-high heat.
4. Spray the grill grate with oil mist.
5. Lay out the shrimp onto the grill and cook for around 2-3 minutes from both sides.
6. Shift the shrimp onto a platter and let them cool slightly.
7. For the dressing: put yogurt and remnant ingredients into a small-sized bowl, and merge to incorporate.
8. Place lettuce and shrimp into a large-sized salad bowl and drizzle with dressing.
9. Top with Parmesan cheese and enjoy right away.

Ingredients

For the Shrimp:
One and quarter lb. shrimp - Two tbsp. olive oil - Six cloves garlic, finely cut up - One tsp. lemon zest, grated - One tsp. salt - Half tsp. powdered black pepper
For the Caesar Dressing:
Half C. fat-free plain Greek yogurt - One third C. Parmesan cheese, grated - Two tbsp. balsamic vinegar - Two tbsp. olive oil - Two cloves garlic - One tsp. sal - One tsp. powdered black pepper
For the Salad:
Three romaine lettuce heads, cut in half lengthwise
One third C. Parmesan cheese, shredded

NUTRITIONAL VALUES : TOTAL CALORIES: 316; TOTAL CARBOHYDRATES: 6.7G; DIETARY FIBER: 0.1G; SUGARS: 2.5G; PROTEIN: 40G; TOTAL FAT: 13.6G; SATURATED FAT: 4.4G

Ratatouille

🕐 **Prep:** *20 mins*   📷 **Cook:** *45 mins*   🍽 **Serves:** *4*

Directions

1. For preheating: set your oven at 375ºF.
2. Put the tomato paste, one tbsp. of oil, onion, garlic, salt and pepper into a bowl and merge nicely.
3. Place the tomato paste mixture in the bottom of a 10x10-inch baking pan and spread.
4. Lay out alternating vegetable slices into the baking pan.
5. Drizzle the vegetables with the remnant oil and then sprinkle with salt and pepper, followed by the thyme.
6. Arrange a piece of bakery paper over the vegetables.
7. Bake in your oven for around 45 minutes.
8. Enjoy right away.

Ingredients

Six oz. tomato paste - Three tbsp. olive oil, divided - Half onion, cut up - Three tbsp. garlic, finely cut up - Salt and powdered black pepper, as desired - Three quarters C. water - One zucchini, slivered into thin circles - One yellow squash, slivered into circles thinly - One eggplant, slivered into circles thinly - Two bell peppers (multi-colored), seeded and slivered into circles thinly - One tbsp. fresh thyme leaves, finely cut up - One tbsp. fresh lemon juice

NUTRITIONAL VALUES : TOTAL CALORIES: 206; TOTAL CARBOHYDRATES: 26.4G; DIETARY FIBER: 8.4G; SUGARS: 14.1G; PROTEIN: 5.4G; TOTAL FAT: 11.4G; SATURATED FAT: 2.3G

Tuna & Apple
Sandwiches

🕐 **Prep:** *10 mins*   🍽 **Serves:** *1*

Directions

1. Put the tuna, apple, yogurt, mustard and honey into a bowl and merge to incorporate.
2. Spread about half C. of the tuna mixture over each of 3 bread slices.
3. Top each sandwich with 1 lettuce leaf.
4. Close with the remnant 3 bread slices.
5. Cut the sandwiches in half and enjoy right away.

Ingredients

One (fifteen-oz.) can water-packed tuna, drained - One medium-sized apple, peel removed, cored and cut up - Three tbsp. plain Greek yogurt - One tsp. mustard - Half tsp. honey - Four whole-wheat bread slices - Two lettuce leaves

NUTRITIONAL VALUES : TOTAL CALORIES: 283; TOTAL CARBOHYDRATES: 40.2G; DIETARY FIBER: G; SUGARS: 16.4G; PROTEIN: 26.6G; TOTAL FAT: 4G; SATURATED FAT: 0.1G

Cold Sesame Noodle
Salad with Veggies

🕐 **Prep:** *20 mins*   🍲 **Cook:** *10 mins*   🍽 **Serves:** *4*

Directions

1. For the dressing: put tamari and remnant ingredients into a small-sized bowl and whisk to incorporate. Put it aside.
2. Cook the noodles into a large-sized cooking pot of boiling water for around 8-10 minutes.
3. Drain the pasta and rinse thoroughly.
4. Put noodles and remnant ingredients into a large-sized salad bowl and merge to incorporate.
5. Place the dressing over salad and merge to incorporate.
6. Enjoy right away.

Ingredients

For the Dressing:
Quarter C. tamari - Three tbsp. sesame oil, toasted - Two tbsp. balsamic vinegar - One tbsp. fresh lime juice - One tbsp. sesame seeds, toasted - Two cloves garlic, finely cut up - One tbsp. ginger paste - Two tbsp. Erythritol - Quarter tsp. red chili pepper flakes
For the Salad:
Twelve oz. whole-wheat noodles - Half C. snap peas, slivered - Half C. frozen shelled edamame, thawed - Half C. carrots, peel removed and shredded - Half C. fresh cilantro, cut up - Half red pepper, seeded then julienned - Quarter cucumber, julienned - Two scallions, cut up

NUTRITIONAL VALUES : TOTAL CALORIES: 436; TOTAL CARBOHYDRATES: 58.3G; DIETARY FIBER: 3.6G; SUGARS: 3.3G; PROTEIN: 16.7G; TOTAL FAT: 15.6G; SATURATED FAT: 2.2G

Tofu & Snap Pea Sauté
With Ginger Soy Sauce

🕐 **Prep:** *20 mins*   📠 **Cook:** *12 mins*   🍽 **Serves:** *3*

Directions

1. For the sauce: put the garlic and remnant ingredients into a small-sized bowl and merge to incorporate. Put it aside.
2. Sizzle olive oil into a large-sized wok on burner at high heat.
3. Put in tofu and cook for around 3 minutes, without stirring.
4. Flip and sear for around 2-3 minutes.
5. With the spoon, move the tofu to one side of wok.
6. Add sugar snap peas and scallions and stir-fry for around 2 minutes.
7. Put in sauce and cook for around 2 minutes.
8. Blend the tofu with sauce mixture and cook for around 1-2 minutes.
9. Enjoy right away.

Ingredients

For the Sauce:
Four cloves garlic, grated - Two small-sized jalapeño peppers, seeded and thinly slivered - One and half tbsp. soy sauce - One and half tsp. fresh ginger, grated - One and half tbsp. fresh lime juice - One and half tsp. sesame oil, toasted - One and half tsp. red boat fish sauce
One tsp. honey
For the Tofu Mixture:
One (fourteen-oz.) package extra-firm tofu, pressed, drained and cubed - Two tbsp. olive oil - Six oz. sugar snap peas, trimmed and thinly slivered - Three scallions, thinly slivered

NUTRITIONAL VALUES ; TOTAL CALORIES: 362; TOTAL CARBOHYDRATES: 35G; DIETARY FIBER: 4G; SUGARS: 18G; PROTEIN: 18G; TOTAL FAT: 19G; SATURATED FAT: 3G

Creamy Broccoli
& Almond Soup

🕐 **Prep:** *15 mins*   📠 **Cook:** *45 mins*   🍽 **Serves:** *4*

Directions

1. In a large-sized soup pan, sizzle the oil on burner at moderate heat.
2. Cook the onion for around 4-5 minutes.
3. Put in garlic, thyme and spices and sauté for around 1 minute more.
4. Put in broccoli and cook for around 3-4 minutes.
5. Blend in the broth and immediately turn the heat at high.
6. Cook the mixture until boiling.
7. Immediately turn the heat at medium-low.
8. Cover the soup pan and cook for around 32-35 minutes.
9. Take off from burner and put to one side to cool slightly.
10. In a mixer, place the mixture in batches with avocado and whirl to form a perfectly silky mixture.
11. Enjoy right away.

Ingredients

Two tbsp. olive oil - Half C. onion, cut up - One clove garlic, finely cut up - One tbsp. fresh thyme, cut up - Quarter tsp. powdered cumin - Quarter tsp. red pepper flakes - Fifteen raw almonds - Two medium-sized heads broccoli, cut into florets - Four C. vegetable broth - One avocado, peel removed, pitted and cut up

TOTAL CALORIES: 260; TOTAL CARBOHYDRATES: 16.8G; DIETARY FIBER: 7.3G; SUGARS: 3.8G; PROTEIN: 9.7G; TOTAL FAT: 18.7G; SATURATED FAT: 3.5G

Greek Salad
With Grilled Chicken Strips

🕐 **Prep:** *20* mins   🍲 **Cook:** *14* mins   🍽 **Serves:** *4*

Directions

1. For the chicken: in a glass-baking pan, put the vinegar, oil, lemon juice and seasoning and merge thoroughly.
2. Put in chicken breasts and coat with the mixture.
3. Shift into your refrigerator to marinate for around 25-30 minutes.
4. For preheating: set your grill to moderate heat.
5. Spray the grill grate.
6. Take off the chicken breasts from the bowl and discard the remnant marinade.
7. Lay out the chicken breasts onto the grill and cover with the lid.
8. Cook for around 5-7 minutes from both sides.
9. In the meantime, for the dressing: put the oil and remnant ingredients into a bowl and whisk to incorporate.
10. Take off the chicken breasts from grill and shift onto a chopping block for around 9-10 minutes.
11. Cut each cooked chicken breast into slices.
12. For the salad: put the lettuce and remnant ingredients into a large-sized salad bowl and merge thoroughly.
13. Top with chicken slices and drizzle with dressing.
14. Enjoy right away.

Ingredients

For the Chicken:
Four cloves garlic, grated - Two tbsp. balsamic vinegar - Two tbsp. olive oil - One tsp. fresh lemon juice - Half tsp. lemon-pepper seasoning - Two (six-oz.) boneless chicken breast, pounded slightly

For the Salad:
One lettuce head, shredded - One large-sized cucumber, slivered - One C. cherry tomatoes, halved - Half C. kalamata olives, pitted - Quarter C. feta cheese, crumbled

For the Dressing:
Three tbsp. olive oil - One tbsp. balsamic vinegar - Half tsp. dried oregano - Half tsp. salt

NUTRITIONAL VALUES : TOTAL CALORIES: 359; TOTAL CARBOHYDRATES: 8.7G; DIETARY FIBER: 2.1G; SUGARS: 3.7G; PROTEIN: 27.4G; TOTAL FAT: 24.5G; SATURATED FAT: 5.4G

Lemon Tilapia
With Roasted Broccoli

🕐 **Prep:** *10 mins*   🔲 **Cook:** *20 mins*   🍽 **Serves:** *6*

Directions

1. For preheating: set your oven at 375°F.
2. Spray a shallow baking pan with oil mist.
3. Put tilapia fillets, oil, lemon juice, Old Bay seasoning and garlic salt into a bowl and merge to incorporate.
4. Place out the tilapia fillets into the baking pan.
5. Lay out the broccoli around the fillets.
6. Bake in your oven for around 20 minutes.
7. Enjoy right away.

Ingredients

Anti-sticking oil mist - One tbsp. olive oil - Six (four-oz.) frozen tilapia fillets, thawed - Two tbsp. Old Bay seasoning - Two tbsp. lemon juice - Half tbsp. garlic salt - One (twelve-oz.) package frozen broccoli

NUTRITIONAL VALUES : TOTAL CALORIES: 133; TOTAL CARBOHYDRATES: 3.8G; DIETARY FIBER: 1.3G; SUGARS: 1.1G; PROTEIN: 22.6G; TOTAL FAT: 3.6G; SATURATED FAT: 0.8G

Herb-Crusted Baked
Salmon with Lemon Asparagus

🕐 **Prep:** *15 mins*   🔲 **Cook:** *9 mins*   🍽 **Serves:** *4*

Directions

1. For preheating: set your oven at 450°F.
2. For the salmon: put salmon and remnant ingredients into a large-sized salad bowl and gently toss to incorporate.
3. Sizzle an ovenproof wok on burner at moderate heat.
4. Cook the salmon fillets for around 2 minutes, without touching.
5. Flip the fillets and immediately shift the wok into the oven.
6. Bake in your oven for around 6-7 minutes.
7. In the meantime, for the asparagus: sizzle oil into a large-sized cast-iron wok on burner at moderate heat.
8. Cook the asparagus with salt, and pepper for around 5-6 minutes.
9. Blend in the garlic and lemon zest.
10. Cook for around 1-2 minutes, blending frequently.
11. Blend in lemon juice and take off from burner.
12. Cut each salmon fillet in 2 portions and enjoy alongside the asparagus.

Ingredients

For the Salmon:
Two (eight-oz.) boneless salmon fillets - Two tbsp. olive oil - One tsp. fresh rosemary, cut up - One tsp. fresh thyme, cut up - One tsp. fresh oregano, cut up - Salt and powdered black pepper, as desired
For the Asparagus:
One tbsp. olive oil - Sixteen oz. asparagus, trimmed - Salt and powdered black pepper, as desired - Two garlic cloves, finely cut up - Half tsp. lemon zest, grated - Two tbsp. lemon juice

NUTRITIONAL VALUES : TOTAL CALORIES: 270; TOTAL CARBOHYDRATES: 5.7G; DIETARY FIBER: 2.8G; SUGARS: 2.3G; PROTEIN: 24.7G; TOTAL FAT: 17.8G; SATURATED FAT: 2.7G

Spaghetti Squash Primavera
With Olive Oil Drizzle

🕐 **Prep:** *15 mins* 🍲 **Cook:** *55 mins* 🍽 **Serves:** *6*

Directions

1. For preheating: set your oven at 350ºF.
2. Lay out the squash halves into a baking pan, cut-side-up.
3. Drizzle squash halves with one tbsp. of oil and sprinkle with salt.
4. Bake in your oven for around 35-40 minutes.
5. Take off the baking pan from oven and with a fork, separate the flesh into strands.
6. Shift the squash noodles into a medium-sized bowl. Put to one side.
7. Sizzle one tbsp. of the olive oil into a large-sized wok on burner at moderate-low heat.
8. Cook the garlic for around 2 minutes.
9. Put in broccoli and cook for around 8 minutes.
10. Blend in the mushrooms, fresh herbs and red pepper flakes.
11. Cook for around 3 minutes.
12. Blend in tomatoes and olives.
13. Cook for around 2 minutes.
14. Shift the mixture into the bowl with the squash noodles.
15. Put in remnant oil, salt and pepper and merge to incorporate.
16. Decorate with pine nuts and enjoy right away.

Ingredients

One medium-sized spaghetti squash, halved and seeded - Three tbsp. olive oil, divided - Sea salt, as desired - Four cloves garlic, finely cut up - Two and half C. small-sized broccoli florets - One C. oyster mushrooms, slivered - Two and half tsp. fresh rosemary, cut up - One tsp. fresh thyme, cut up - One pinch of red pepper flakes - One C. cherry tomatoes, halved - Quarter C. green olives, pitted and cut up - Powdered black pepper , as desired - Quarter C. pine nuts, lightly toasted

NUTRITIONAL VALUES : TOTAL CALORIES: 135; TOTAL CARBOHYDRATES: 12G; DIETARY FIBER: 3G; SUGARS: 4G; PROTEIN: 3G; TOTAL FAT: 10G; SATURATED FAT: 1G

Seared Cod
With Tomato & Olives

🕐 **Prep:** *10 mins* 🍲 **Cook:** *10 mins* 🍽 **Serves:** *4*

Directions

1. Sprinkle the cod fillets with salt and pepper.
2. Sizzle oil into a large-sized anti-sticking cooking pot on burner at moderate heat.
3. Cook the cod fillets for around 5 minutes.
4. Flip the cod the fillets and cook for around 2 minutes.
5. Put in the onion and garlic and cook for around 2 minutes.
6. Put in the tomatoes, olives, wine and lemon juice.
7. Cook for around 2 minutes.
8. Decorate with parsley and enjoy right away.

Ingredients

Four skinless cod fillets - One pinch of salt - Cracked black pepper, as desired - Two tbsp. olive oil - Two large-sized cloves garlic, finely cut up - One onion, finely slivered - One C. cherry tomatoes, quartered - One third C. pitted kalamata olives - Quarter C. white wine - One tbsp. lemon juice - Two tbsp. fresh parsley, cut up

NUTRITIONAL VALUES : TOTAL CALORIES: 396; TOTAL CARBOHYDRATES: 3G; DIETARY FIBER: 0.1G; SUGARS: 1G; PROTEIN: 16G; TOTAL FAT: 6G; SATURATED FAT: 1G

Cilantro Lime Chicken
With Zucchini Noodles

🕐 **Prep:** *20 mins*   ▦ **Cook:** *12 mins*   🍽 **Serves:** *4*

Directions

1. With a fork, pierce chicken breasts several times
2. In a large-sized bowl, put the garlic and remnant ingredients except the chicken breasts and merge to incorporate thoroughly.
3. Put in chicken breasts and coat with the marinade.
4. Shift into your refrigerator to marinate for around 2-3 hours.
5. For preheating: set your grill to moderate-high heat.
6. Spray the grill grate with oil mist.
7. Take off the chicken from marinade.
8. Lay out the chicken breasts onto the grill.
9. Cook for around 5-6 minutes from both sides.
10. In the meantime, sizzle oil into an anti-sticking wok on burner at moderate heat.
11. Cook the garlic and jalapeño pepper for around 1 minute.
12. Put in zucchini noodles and sauté for around 3-4 minutes.
13. Blend in lime juice, salt and pepper and take off from burner.
14. Enjoy chicken breasts alongside the zucchini noodles.

Ingredients

For the Chicken:
Three cloves garlic, cut up finely - Three tbsp. fresh cilantro, cut up - Three tbsp. olive oil - Three tbsp. lime juice - One tsp. paprika - Half tsp. dried oregano - Salt and powdered black pepper, as desired - Four (four-oz.) boneless chicken breast halves - Anti-sticking oil mist

For the Zucchini Noodles:
One tbsp. olive oil - One garlic clove, finely cut up - Quarter of jalapeño pepper, seeded and cut up - Two large-sized zucchinis, spiralized with Blade C - Half tbsp. fresh lime juice - Salt and powdered black pepper, as desired

NUTRITIONAL VALUES : TOTAL CALORIES: 371; TOTAL CARBOHYDRATES: 7.9G; DIETARY FIBER: 2.2G; SUGARS: 3.2G; PROTEIN: 35.1G; TOTAL FAT: 22.8G; SATURATED FAT: 4.4G

Slow Cooked
Chickpeas Stew

🕐 **Prep:** *17 mins*   ▦ **Cook:** *7 hrs*   🍽 **Serves:** *6*

Directions

1. Put the tomatoes, onion, carrot, garlic, oregano, salt, red pepper flakes, black pepper and broth into a Slow Cooker and merge to incorporate.
2. Close the Slow Cooker with its lid and set on "Low" setting for 6 hours.
3. After cooking time is finished, take off the lid and Shift Quarter C. of the cooking liquid into a small-sized bowl.
4. In the bowl with cooking liquid, put two tbsp. of chickpeas and with a fork, mash to form a perfectly silky mixture.
5. In the slow cooker, put the mashed chickpeas, kale, lemon juice and remnant chickpeas and merge to incorporate.
6. Close the Slow Cooker with its lid and set on "Low" setting for 1 hour.
7. Shift the soup into serving dishes and drizzle each with oil.
8. Enjoy right away.

Ingredients

Two (fourteen-oz.) cans fire-roasted diced tomatoes - One C. onion, cut up - Three quarters C. carrot, peel removed and cut up - Four cloves garlic, finely cut up - One tsp. dried oregano - Half tsp. red pepper flakes - Salt and powdered black pepper, as desired - Three C. reduced-sodium vegetable broth - One (fifteen-oz.) can chickpeas, drained and divided - Eight C. fresh kale, tough ribs removed and cut up - One tbsp. lemon juice - Three tbsp. olive oil

NUTRITIONAL VALUES : TOTAL CALORIES: 238; TOTAL CARBOHYDRATES: 35.1G; DIETARY FIBER: 7G; SUGARS: 5.1G; PROTEIN: 8.9G; TOTAL FAT: 8.2G; SATURATED FAT: 3.1G

Rosemary Lamb Chops
With Steamed Green Beans

🕐 **Prep:** *15 mins*　　🍲 **Cook:** *8 mins*　　🍽 **Serves:** *4*

Directions

1. Place the cloves garlic onto a chopping block and sprinkle with some salt.
2. With a knife, crush the garlic until paste forms.
3. Shift the garlic paste into a bowl.
4. Put in rosemary, salt and pepper and merge thoroughly.
5. With a sharp knife, make 3-4 cuts on both sides of the chops.
6. Rub the chops with garlic mixture.
7. Sizzle one tbsp. of oil into a large-sized cast-iron wok on burner at moderate heat.
8. Cook the chops for around 3 minutes from both sides.
9. In the meantime, in a large-sized cooking pot of boiling water, arranger a steamer insert.
10. Lay out the green beans into the steamer insert.
11. Steam with the cover for around 4-5 minutes.
12. Take off the steamer insert and drain the green beans thoroughly.
13. In a bowl, put green beans, oil, salt and pepper and merge to incorporate.
14. Drizzle with lemon juice and enjoy right away.

Ingredients

Four cloves garlic, peel removed - Salt, as desired - Three-four tbsp. fresh rosemary, finely cut up - Powdered black pepper, as desired - Eight (four-oz.) lamb chops, trimmed - Two tbsp. olive oil, divided - One tbsp. fresh lemon juice - One lb. of fresh green beans, trimmed - Salt and powdered black pepper, as desired

NUTRITIONAL VALUES : TOTAL CALORIES: 531; **TOTAL CARBOHYDRATES:** 10.8G; **DIETARY FIBER:** 5G; **SUGARS:** 1.7G; **PROTEIN:** 66.1G; **TOTAL FAT:** 24.2G; **SATURATED FAT:** 7.2G

Pesto & Mozzarella
Stuffed Chicken Breasts

🕐 **Prep:** *15 mins*　📟 **Cook:** *40 mins*　🍽 **Serves:** *4*

Directions

1. For preheating: set your oven at 375ºF.
2. Spray a glass baking pan with oil mist.
3. Place 1 chicken breasts onto a smooth surface.
4. Hold a knife parallel to work surface, slice the chicken breast horizontally, without cutting all the way through.
5. Then open each chicken breast and flatten to resemble butterfly shape.
6. Spread pesto onto each chicken breast and top with 1 mozzarella slice.
7. Wrap chicken around cheese and then secure with toothpicks.
8. In large-sized bowl, put breadcrumbs, salt and pepper and merge to incorporate.
9. Coat chicken with breadcrumb mixture.
10. Lay out the chicken breasts into the baking pan.
11. Bake in your oven for around 30-40 minutes.
12. Cut into slices and enjoy right away.

Ingredients

4 boneless skinless chicken breasts - 1 C. basil pesto - 4 (half-inch thick) mozzarella cheese slices - 1 C. whole-wheat breadcrumbs - 1 tsp. salt - 1 tsp. powdered black pepper

NUTRITIONAL VALUES : TOTAL CALORIES: 498; TOTAL CARBOHYDRATES: 22.4G; DIETARY FIBER: 1.2G; SUGARS: 1.7G; PROTEIN: 41.9G; TOTAL FAT: 26G; SATURATED FAT: 6.3G

Beef & Vegetable
Kabobs with Tzatziki Sauce

🕐 **Prep:** *20 mins*　　🍲 **Cook:** *6 mins*　　🍽 **Serves:** *8*

Directions

1. For the marinade: put oil and remnant ingredients into a large-sized bowl and whisk to incorporate.
2. Put 2 tbsp. of marinade and vegetables into a large-sized bowl and merge to incorporate.
3. Put the beef cubes into the bowl of remnant marinade and merge to incorporate.
4. Shift the bowls of vegetables and beef into your refrigerator for around 4-6 hours.
5. In the meantime, for the tzatziki sauce: arrange a colander in the sink.
6. Place the cucumber into the colander and sprinkle with salt.
7. Let it drain for around 10-15 minutes.
8. With your hands, squeeze the cucumber well.
9. Put the cucumber and remnant ingredients into a large-sized bowl and merge to incorporate.
10. Cover the bowl of cucumber mixture and shift into your refrigerator to chill for around 3-4 hours before enjoying.
11. For preheating: set your grill to moderate-high heat.
12. Spray the grill grate with oil mist.
13. Thread the vegetables and beef cubes onto skewers.
14. Place the skewers of vegetables and beef onto the grill grate and cook for around 2-3 minutes from both sides.
15. Enjoy the kabobs alongside the tzatziki sauce.

Ingredients

For the Marinade:
Quarter C. olive oil - Three tbsp. lemon juice - Two tbsp. balsamic vinegar - One tbsp. dried oregano - Two tsp. paprika - Two tsp. garlic powder - One tsp. onion powder - One tsp. powdered cumin - One tsp. powdered coriander - One tsp. salt - Quarter tsp. powdered black pepper

For the Beef & Veggies:
Two lb. top sirloin, cubed - Two bell peppers, seeded and cubed - Two C. cherry tomatoes - Two small-sized or One large-sized zucchini cut into Quarter" slices - One large-sized red onion, cubed

For the Tzatziki Sauce:
One large-sized English cucumber, peel removed and grated - Salt, as desired - Two C. fat-free plain - Greek yogurt - One tbsp. fresh lemon juice - Four cloves garlic, finely cut up - One tbsp. fresh mint leaves, cut up - Two tbsp. fresh dill, cut up - One pinch of cayenne powder - Powdered black pepper, as desired

NUTRITIONAL VALUES : TOTAL CALORIES: 355; TOTAL CARBOHYDRATES: 14.6G; DIETARY FIBER: 2.6G; SUGARS: 9.4G; PROTEIN: 40G; TOTAL FAT: 14.7G; SATURATED FAT: 4.3G

Cajun Shrimp & Cauliflower
Rice Bowl

🕐 **Prep:** *20 mins*   📠 **Cook:** *12 mins*   🍽 **Serves:** *4*

Directions

1. For the Cajun seasoning: put the dried herbs, spices and salt into a small-sized bowl and merge to incorporate. Put to one side.
2. For the cauliflower rice: sizzle oil into a large-sized wok on burner at moderate heat.
3. Put in cauliflower rice, garlic and half of the Cajun seasoning and merge thoroughly.
4. Cook with the cover for around 5-7 minutes, blending from time to time.
5. For the shrimp: put shrimp, oil and remnant Cajun seasoning into a bowl and merge to incorporate.
6. Place the shrimp into the wok with cauliflower rice and merge to incorporate.
7. Cook with the cover for around 4-5 minutes.
8. Blend in parsley and enjoy right away.

Ingredients

For the Cajun Seasoning:
Half tsp. dried thyme - Half tsp. dried oregano - One tsp. paprika - Half tsp. cayenne powder - One tsp. garlic powder - Half tsp. powdered black pepper - Half tsp. onion powder - Quarter tsp. red pepper flakes - Salt, as desired
For the Cauliflower Rice:
Two tbsp. olive oil - Twenty four oz. cauliflower rice - Two tsp. garlic, finely cut up - Two tbsp. fresh parsley, cut up
For the Shrimp:
One and half lb. medium shrimp, peel removed and deveined One tbsp. olive oil

NUTRITIONAL VALUES : TOTAL CALORIES: 316; TOTAL CARBOHYDRATES: 30G; DIETARY FIBER: 3G; SUGARS: 3G; PROTEIN: 38G; TOTAL FAT: 2G; SATURATED FAT: 2G

Slow-Cooked
Chicken Marsala

🕐 **Prep:** *15 mins*   📠 **Cook:** *6½ hrs*   🍽 **Serves:** *4*

Directions

1. Lightly spray the pot of slow cooker with oil mist.
2. Sprinkle the chicken breasts with salt and pepper.
3. Lay out the chicken breasts into the pot of your slow cooker.
4. Top with garlic, mushrooms, broth and marsala.
5. Close the Slow Cooker with its lid and set on "Low" setting for 6 hours.
6. With a frying ladle, shift chicken breasts onto a plate.
7. Whisk together the water and cornstarch into a small-sized bowl.
8. Place the cornstarch mixture into the slow cooker with chicken mixture and whisk to incorporate.
9. Blend in the cooked chicken.
10. Close the Slow Cooker with its lid and set on "High" setting for 30 minutes.
11. Enjoy right away with a decoration of parsley.

Ingredients

Four (for-oz.) boneless chicken breasts - Salt and powdered black pepper, as desired - Two tsp. garlic, finely cut up - One C. fresh mushrooms, slivered - One C. chicken broth - Quarter C. marsala wine - Quarter C. water - Quarter C. cornstarch - Two tbsp. fresh parsley, roughly cut up

NUTRITIONAL VALUES : TOTAL CALORIES: 170; TOTAL CARBOHYDRATES: 9G; DIETARY FIBER: 1G; SUGARS: 1G; PROTEIN: 25G; TOTAL FAT: 3G; SATURATED FAT: 1G

Vegetarian Chili with Avocado & Sour Cream

🕐 **Prep:** *15 mins*　　📷 **Cook:** *40 mins*　　🍽 **Serves:** *8*

Directions

1. Sizzle the oil into a Dutch oven on burner at moderate heat.
2. Cook the onion and bell pepper for around 5 minutes.
3. Blend in the garlic, oregano and spices and sauté for around 1-2 minutes.
4. Put in pumpkin puree and both cans of tomatoes with juice and with a wire whisk blend thoroughly.
5. Blend in the beans, water, salt and pepper.
6. Cook the mixture until boiling.
7. Immediately turn the heat at low.
8. Cook partially covered for around 30 minutes, blending from time to time.
9. Enjoy right away with the decoration of parsley.

Ingredients

One tbsp. olive oil - One medium-sized white onion, cut up - One bell pepper, seeded and cut up - Two cloves garlic, finely cut up - One tsp. dried oregano - One tbsp. red chili powder - One tsp. powdered cumin - Quarter tsp. powdered cinnamon - One pinch of powdered nutmeg - One (fifteen-oz.) can sugar-free pumpkin puree - Two (fourteen-oz.) cans diced tomatoes with juice - One (fifteen-oz.) can fire-roasted diced tomatoes, with juice - One (fifteen-oz.) can garbanzo beans, drained - One (fifteen-oz.) can black beans, drained - One C. water - Salt and powdered black pepper, as desired - Quarter C. fresh parsley, cut up

NUTRITIONAL VALUES : TOTAL CALORIES: 452; TOTAL CARBOHYDRATES: 79.1G; DIETARY FIBER: 21.7G; SUGARS: 14G; PROTEIN: 24.2G; TOTAL FAT: 6.4G; SATURATED FAT: 0.9G

Honey Mustard Glazed Pork Chops with Apple Slaw

🕐 **Prep:** *15 mins*　　📷 **Cook:** *12 mins*　　🍽 **Serves:** *4*

Directions

1. Sprinkle the pork chops with one tsp. of salt and half tsp. f pepper.
2. Sizzle oil in a large-sized cast-iron wok on burner at moderate-high heat.
3. Cook the pork chops for around 5-6 minutes from both sides.
4. Shift the pork chops onto a plate.
5. In the meantime, in a large-sized bowl, put mayonnaise, vinegar, poppy seeds, hot sauce, remnant salt and pepper and whisk to incorporate.
6. Add apple, celery, parsley and chives and merge to incorporate.
7. Enjoy pork chops alongside the apple slaw.

Ingredients

Four (ten-oz.) bone-in pork chops - One and half tsp. salt, divided - Three quarters tsp. black pepper, divided - One tbsp. olive oil - Three apples, cored and cut into thin sticks - Quarter C. mayonnaise - Four tsp. apple cider vinegar - One tsp. poppy seeds - Quarter tsp. hot sauce - Four celery stalks, thinly slivered - One C. fresh parsley, cut up - One third C. fresh chives

NUTRITIONAL VALUES : TOTAL CALORIES: 519; TOTAL CARBOHYDRATES: 29.6G; DIETARY FIBER: 5G; SUGARS: 20.1G; PROTEIN: 41.6G; TOTAL FAT: 28.1G; SATURATED FAT: 8.4G

Spicy
Tofu with Veggies

🕐 **Prep:** *20 mins*　　🗊 **Cook:** *42 mins*　　🍽 **Serves:** *4*

Directions

1. For preheating: set your oven at 400ºF.
2. Lay out bakery paper onto a large-sized, rimmed baking tray..
3. Lay out the tofu cubes onto the baking tray.
4. Bake in your oven for around 26-30 minutes.
5. In the meantime, in a small-sized bowl, put soy sauce, one tbsp. of the sesame oil, peanut butter, maple syrup, lime juice and chili garlic sauce and whisk to incorporate thoroughly. Put it to one side.
6. Take off from oven and place the tofu cubes into the bowl of sauce.
7. Stir the mixture well and put to one side for around 9-10 minutes, blending from time to time.
8. With a frying ladle, take off the tofu cubes from bowl, reserving the sauce.
9. Sizzle a large-sized, cast-iron wok on burner at moderate heat.
10. Cook the tofu cubes for around 5 minutes, blending from time to time.
11. With a frying ladle, shift the tofu cubes onto a plate. Put to one side.
12. Put the remnant sesame oil, green beans, bell peppers and two-three tbsp. of reserved sauce into the same wok and merge thoroughly.
13. Cook with the cover for around 4-5 minutes.
14. Immediately turn the heat at medium-high and merge in the cooked tofu remnant reserved sauce.
15. Cook for around 1-2 minutes, blending frequently.
16. Blend in the scallion greens and take off from burner.
17. Enjoy right away.

Ingredients

One (fourteen-oz.) package extra firm tofu, pressed, drained and cut into small-sized cubes - Two tbsp. sesame oil, divided - Four tbsp. reduced-sodium soy sauce - Three tbsp. maple syrup - Two tbsp. peanut butter - Two tbsp. fresh lime juice - One-two tsp. chili garlic sauce - One lb. green beans, trimmed - Two-three small-sized bell peppers, seeded and cubed - Two scallion greens, cut up

NUTRITIONAL VALUES : TOTAL CALORIES: 347; TOTAL CARBOHYDRATES: 32G; DIETARY FIBER: 6.6G; SUGARS: 20G; PROTEIN: 17.2G; TOTAL FAT: 19.9G; SATURATED FAT: 3.7G

Parmesan Crusted
Tilapia with Broccoli

🕐 **Prep:** *15 mins*　　🍲 **Cook:** *10 mins*　　🍽 **Serves:** *6*

Directions

1. For preheating: set your oven to broiler.
2. Spray a broiler pan with oil mist.
3. For the broccoli: lay out a steamer insert into a large-sized cooking pot of water.
4. Cook the water until boiling.
5. Lay out the broccoli into the steamer insert and cook with the cover for around 8-10 minutes.
6. Drain the broccoli and Shift onto a plate.
7. Sprinkle the broccoli with salt.
8. For the tilapia: in a large-sized bowl, put Parmesan cheese and remnant ingredients except for tilapia fillets and merge to incorporate. Put it to one side.
9. Place the fillets onto broiler pan.
10. Broil the fillets for around 2-3 minutes.
11. Take off the broiler pan from oven and top the fillets with cheese mixture.
12. Broil for around 2 minutes further.
13. Enjoy tilapia alongside the broccoli.

Ingredients

For the Broccoli:
One lb. broccoli, cut into florets - Salt, as desired

For the Tilapia:
Olive oil mist - Half C. Parmesan cheese, grated - Three tbsp. mayonnaise - Quarter C. unsalted butter, softened - Two tbsp. fresh lemon juice - Quarter tsp. dried thyme - Salt and powdered black pepper, as desired - Four (four-oz.) tilapia fillets

NUTRITIONAL VALUES : TOTAL CALORIES: 190; TOTAL CARBOHYDRATES: 3.4G; DIETARY FIBER: 1.2G; SUGARS: 1.4G; PROTEIN: 24.2G; TOTAL FAT: 9.8G; SATURATED FAT: 2.3G

Balsamic Glazed Beef Stir Fry
With Mixed Veggies

🕐 **Prep:** *20 mins*   🍲 **Cook:** *15 mins*   🍽 **Serves:** *4*

Ingredients

Directions

1. Put broth, soy sauce, vinegar, honey and cornstarch into a bowl and merge to incorporate. Put it to one side.
2. Sizzle half of oil into a large-sized wok on burner at moderate-high heat.
3. Cook the ginger for around 15 seconds.
4. Put in peppers and onions and cook for around 4 minutes.
5. Blend in garlic, bok choy and mushrooms and cook for around 3 minutes.
6. With a frying ladle, shift the cooked vegetables into a bowl.
7. Sizzle remnant oil into the same wok on burner at around moderate-high heat.
8. Cook the beef slices for around 2-3 minutes.
9. Push beef to one side of the wok.
10. Place the sauce in the center of wok.
11. Cook for around 1 minute.
12. Blend in cooked vegetables and cook for around 1 minute.
13. Enjoy right away.

Twelve oz. top sirloin steak, thinly slivered - Three quarters C. beef broth - Two tbsp. reduced-sodium soy sauce - Two tbsp. balsamic vinegar - Two tbsp. honey - Two tbsp. cornstarch - Three tbsp. olive oil, divided - One tbsp. fresh ginger, finely cut up - Two small-sized bell peppers, seeded and cut into thin strips - One yellow onion, thinly slivered - Three cloves garlic, finely cut up - One lb. baby bok choy, cut up - One C. fresh mushrooms, slivered

NUTRITIONAL VALUES : TOTAL CALORIES: 314; TOTAL CARBOHYDRATES: 25G; DIETARY FIBER: 3G; SUGARS: 15G; PROTEIN: 23G; TOTAL FAT: 14G; SATURATED FAT: 10G

Classic Meatloaf with Spinach
Feta Stuffing

🕐 **Prep:** *20 mins*   📟 **Cook:** *1 hr*   🍽 **Serves:** *4*

Directions

1. For preheating: set your oven at 350°F.
2. Spray a bread mold with oil mist.
3. Sizzle olive oil in a wok on burner at moderate-low heat.
4. Cook the onion for around 4-5 minutes.
5. Shift 2/3 of the onion to a bowl to cool.
6. Blend in half of garlic.
7. Add spinach into the wok and cook for around 1-2 minutes.
8. Take off from burner and let the mixture cool slightly.
9. Blend in sun-dried tomatoes, feta, salt and pepper.
10. Blend in egg white and put it to one side.
11. In the bowl of onion, add egg, breadcrumbs, milk, two tbsp. of tomato sauce, herbs, salt, pepper and remnant garlic and merge thoroughly.
12. Put in ground turkey and merge to incorporate.
13. Place 2/3 of the meat mixture in the bread mold and with a spoon, create a small-sized well in the center.
14. Place the spinach mixture in the well and top with remnant ground turkey.
15. Bake in your oven for around 50-55 minutes.
16. After 30 minutes of cooking, top the meatloaf with tomato sauce.
17. Take off the bread mold from oven and let it rest for around 5-8 minutes before enjoying.

Ingredients

Anti-sticking oil mist - Two tbsp. olive oil - One small-sized onion, finely cut up - Four cloves garlic, finely cut up and divided - One (ten-oz.) bag frozen cut up spinach, thawed and squeezed - Two tbsp. sun-dried tomatoes, cut up - Half C. reduced-fat feta cheese, crumbled - One tsp. salt - Powdered black pepper, as desired - One egg white - One large-sized egg - Three quarters C. whole-wheat breadcrumbs - Quarter C. fat-free milk - One (eight-oz.) can tomato sauce, divided - One tsp. dried basil - One tsp. dried oregano - Quarter C. fresh parsley, cut up - One lb. lean ground turkey

NUTRITIONAL VALUES : TOTAL CALORIES: 639; TOTAL CARBOHYDRATES: 27G; DIETARY FIBER: 4G; SUGARS: 6G; PROTEIN: 45G; TOTAL FAT: 25G; SATURATED FAT: 11G

Hearty Asparagus
Risotto

🕐 **Prep:** *15 mins*   📳 **Cook:** *45 mins*   🍽 **Serves:** *4*

Directions

1. Cook the asparagus into a medium-sized cooking pot of boiling water for around 2-3 minutes.
2. Drain the asparagus and then rinse thoroughly. Put to one side.
3. In a large-sized cooking pot, sizzle oil on burner at moderate heat.
4. Cook the onion for around t 4-5 minutes.
5. Put in garlic and stir-fry for around 1 minute.
6. Put in rice and stir-fry for around 2 minutes.
7. Put in lemon zest, juice and wine and cook for around 2-3 minutes, blending gently.
8. Add 1 C. of broth and cook until all the broth is absorbed, blending from time to time.
9. Repeat this process by adding ¾ C. of broth at one time, blending from time to time till all the broth is absorbed. (This procedure will take about 20-30 minutes)
10. Blend in the cooked asparagus and remnant ingredients and cook for around 3-4 minutes.
11. Enjoy right away.

Ingredients

Fifteen-twenty fresh asparagus spears, trimmed and cut into pieces - Two tbsp. olive oil - One shallot, cut up - One C. onion, cut up - One clove garlic, minced - One C. Arborio rice - One tbsp. lemon zest, grated finely - Two tbsp. fresh lemon juice - Half C. white wine - Five C. hot vegetable broth - One tbsp. fresh parsley, cut up - Quarter C. Parmesan cheese, shredded - Salt and powdered black pepper, as desired

NUTRITIONAL VALUES : TOTAL CALORIES: 241; TOTAL CARBOHYDRATES: 31.8G; DIETARY FIBER: 2.6G; SUGARS: 2.9G; PROTEIN: 9.1G; TOTAL FAT: 6.9G; SATURATED FAT: 1.2G

Tomato Basil Soup
With Grilled Cheese Croutons

🕐 **Prep:** *15 mins*   📳 **Cook:** *15 mins*   🍽 **Serves:** *4*

Directions

1. In a large-sized soup pan, sizzle the oil on burner at moderate heat.
2. Cook the onion alongside the garlic for around 5-6 minutes.
3. Put in tomatoes and cook for around 6-8 minutes, crushing with the back of the spoon from time to time.
4. Blend in the basil, salt and cayenne powder and take off from burner.
5. With a hand blender, puree the soup mixture to form a perfectly silky mixture.
6. In the meantime, for the croutons: spread the mayonnaise onto one side of each bread slice.
7. Place the bread slices onto a chopping block, mayo side-down.
8. Spread cheese over each slice and place remnant bread slices mayo side-up on top to make 2 sandwiches.
9. Sizzle a large-sized, anti-sticking wok on burner at moderate-low heat.
10. Cook the sandwiches for around 4 minutes from both sides.
11. Take off from burner and then cut each sandwich into 1-inch squares.
12. Enjoy the soup with the decoration of croutons.

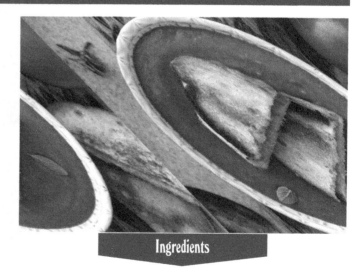

Ingredients

For the Soup:
Two tsp. olive oil - One medium-sized white onion, cut up - Three cloves garlic, finely cut up - Seven C. fresh plum tomatoes, cut up - Half C. fresh basil, cut up - Salt and powdered black pepper, as desired - Quarter tsp. cayenne powder
For the Croutons:
Four whole-grain bread slices - Half C. reduced-fat cheddar cheese, grated - One tbsp. mayonnaise

NUTRITIONAL VALUES : TOTAL CALORIES: 215; TOTAL CARBOHYDRATES: 26.4G; DIETARY FIBER: 5.1G; SUGARS: 15G; PROTEIN: 9.2G; TOTAL FAT: 9.6G; SATURATED FAT: 3.6G

Meatballs & Pasta
Soup

🕐 **Prep:** *20 mins*   🍲 **Cook:** *30 mins*   🍽 **Serves:** *6*

Directions

1. For meatballs: put pork and remnant ingredients except for oil into a bowl and merge to incorporate thoroughly.
2. Shape the meat mixture into balls.
3. Sizzle the oil into a large-sized anti-sticking wok on burner at moderate-high heat.
4. Cook the meatballs in 2 batches for around 4 minutes, flipping from time to time.
5. Shift the meatballs onto a plate lined with paper towels.
6. For soup: sizzle the oil into a large-sized soup pan on burner at moderate-high heat.
7. Cook the onion, carrots and celery for around 6-8 minutes.
8. Put in garlic and cook for around 1 minute.
9. Blend in the broth, salt and pepper and cook until boiling.
10. Put in pasta and meatballs and gently stir to blend.
11. Immediately turn the heat at medium-low.
12. Cook with the cover for around 8 minutes, blending from time to time.
13. Blend in the spinach and cook with the cover for around 2 minutes.
14. Enjoy right away with the decoration of Parmesan cheese.

Ingredients

For the Meatballs:
Eight oz. lean ground pork - Eight oz. lean ground beef - Half C. whole-wheat breadcrumbs - Quarter C. fresh parsley, cut up - One and half tsp. fresh oregano - Half C. Parmesan cheese, shredded finely - One large-sized egg - Salt and powdered black pepper, as desired - One tbsp. olive oil

For the Soup:
One tbsp. olive oil - One and quarter C. yellow onion, cut up - One and quarter C. carrots, peel removed and cut up - Three quarters C. celery, cut up - Four cloves garlic, finely cut up - Five (fourteen and half-oz.) cans reduced-sodium chicken broth - Salt and powdered black pepper, as desired - One C. dry orzo pasta - Six oz. fresh spinach, cut up - One third C. Parmesan cheese, shredded finely

NUTRITIONAL VALUES : TOTAL CALORIES: 408; TOTAL CARBOHYDRATES: 53.6G; DIETARY FIBER: 5.1G; SUGARS: 6G; PROTEIN: 17.1G; TOTAL FAT: 10.4G; SATURATED FAT: 3.1G

Creamed Spinach with Nutmeg
And White Pepper

🕐 **Prep:** *10 mins*   🍲 **Cook:** *16 mins*   🍽 **Serves:** *4*

Directions

1. Sizzle coconut oil into a large-sized wok on burner at moderate heat.
2. Cook the onion for around 8 minutes.
3. Put in frozen spinach and cook for around 5 minutes.
4. Put in coconut milk, cheese, spices, salt and white pepper and merge.
5. Cook for around 2-3 minutes.
6. Enjoy right away.

Ingredients

Three tbsp. coconut oil - One onion, cut up - Sixteen oz. frozen chopped spinach - One C. unsweetened coconut milk - Three quarters part-skim mozzarella cheese - Quarter tsp. powdered nutmeg - Half tsp. garlic powder - Half tsp. powdered white pepper - Salt, as desired

NUTRITIONAL VALUES : TOTAL CALORIES: 175; TOTAL CARBOHYDRATES: 11G; DIETARY FIBER: 3G; SUGARS: 3G; PROTEIN: 7G; TOTAL FAT: 13G; SATURATED FAT: 3G

Lemony Steamed
Green Beans

🕐 **Prep:** *10 mins*   🍲 **Cook:** *5 mins*   🍽 **Serves:** *4*

Directions

1. Lay out a steamer insert into a large-sized cooking pot of boiling water.
2. Lay out the green beans into the steamer insert.
3. Steam with the cover for around 4-5 minutes.
4. Take off the steamer insert and drain the green beans thoroughly.
5. Shift the green beans into a bowl with the remnant ingredients and gently merge.
6. Enjoy right away.

Ingredients

One lb. of fresh green beans, trimmed - One tbsp. of freshly squeezed lemon juice, plus - One tbsp. of lemon zest, grated - One tbsp. of olive oil - One pinch of salt - Powdered black pepper, as per taste

NUTRITIONAL VALUES : TOTAL CALORIES: 67; TOTAL CARBOHYDRATES: 8.5G; DIETARY FIBER: 4G; SUGARS: 1.8G; PROTEIN: 2.1G; TOTAL FAT: 3.7G; SATURATED FAT: 1.1 G

Garlic & Parmesan
Roasted Asparagus

🕐 **Prep:** *10 mins*   ▣ **Cook:** *7 mins*   🍽 **Serves:** *4*

Directions

1. For preheating: set your oven at 425ºF.
2. Put the oil, lemon juice, garlic, salt and pepper into a large-sized bowl and whisk to incorporate.
3. Put in asparagus and merge to incorporate.
4. In another bowl, blend the breadcrumbs and Parmesan cheese.
5. Lay out the asparagus onto a baking tray and sprinkle with cheese mixture.
6. Roast in your oven for around 7 minutes.
7. Enjoy right away.

Ingredients

One tbsp. olive oil - Juice of 1 lemon - One clove garlic finely cut up - Half tsp. kosher salt - Quarter tsp. black pepper - One lb. asparagus, trimmed - Quarter C. whole-wheat breadcrumbs - Quarter C. Parmesan cheese, grated

NUTRITIONAL VALUES : TOTAL CALORIES: 100; TOTAL CARBOHYDRATES: 9G; DIETARY FIBER: 3G; SUGARS: 3G; PROTEIN: 5G; TOTAL FAT: 6G; SATURATED FAT: 2G

Sweet Potato Wedges
With Cilantro Lime Dip

🕐 **Prep:** *15 mins*   ▣ **Cook:** *25 mins*   🍽 **Serves:** *4*

Directions

1. For preheating: set your oven at 425ºF.
2. Lay out a piece of heavy-duty foil onto a baking tray.
3. For the fries: put sweet potato wedges and remnant ingredients into a large-sized bowl, and merge to incorporate.
4. Shift the sweet potato wedges onto the baking tray and spread into an even layer.
5. Bake in your oven for 25 minutes, flipping once after 15 minutes.
6. In the meantime, for the dip: in a bowl, put all ingredients and merge to incorporate.
7. Enjoy the fries alongside the dip.

Ingredients

For the Sweet Potato Fries:
Two large-sized sweet potatoes, peel removed and cut into wedges - Two tsp. powdered turmeric - Two tsp. powdered cinnamon - Sea salt and powdered black pepper, as desired - Three tbsp. olive oil
For the Dip:
One C. fat-free plain Greek yogurt - Three tbsp. fresh cilantro, finely cut up - One tbsp. fresh mint, finely cut up - 2 tbsp. fresh lime juice - Two tsp. honey - Salt, as desired

NUTRITIONAL VALUES : TOTAL CALORIES: 231; TOTAL CARBOHYDRATES: 30.3G; DIETARY FIBER: 4.1G; SUGARS: 8G; PROTEIN: 4.9G; TOTAL FAT: 10.9G; SATURATED FAT: 1.6G

Zesty Quinoa with Corn
& Black Beans

🕐 **Prep:** *15 mins*　　🍽 **Serves:** *6*

Directions

1. For the dressing: put lime juice and remnant ingredients except oil into a mixer and whirl to incorporate thoroughly.
2. Put in oil and whirl to form a perfectly silky mixture.
3. For salad: put the mango and one tbsp. of lime juice into a bowl and merge to incorporate.
4. In another bowl, put the avocado, one pinch of salt and remnant lime juice and merge to incorporate.
5. Put all salad ingredients into a large-sized serving dish and merge to incorporate.
6. Place the dressing and merge to incorporate.
7. Enjoy right away.

Ingredients

For the Dressing:
Quarter C. fresh lime juice - Two tbsp. maple syrup - One tbsp. Dijon mustard - Half tsp. powdered cumin - One tsp. garlic powder - Salt and powdered black pepper, as desired - Half C. olive oil

For the Salad:
Two avocado, peel removed, pitted and cubed - Two tbsp. fresh lime juice, divided - One pinch of salt - One C. cooked quinoa - Two (fourteen-oz.) cans black beans, drained - 1 (fifteen-oz.) can corn, drained - One large-sized bell pepper, seeded and cut up - One small-sized red onion, cut up - 1 jalapeño, seeded and cut up finely - Half C. fresh cilantro, cut up

NUTRITIONAL VALUES : TOTAL CALORIES: 511; TOTAL CARBOHYDRATES: 61.9G; DIETARY FIBER: 15.9G; SUGARS: 7.7G; PROTEIN: 15.3G; TOTAL FAT: 7.7G; SATURATED FAT: 4.1G

Chilled Cucumber Salad
With Dill & Yogurt Dressing

🕐 **Prep:** *15 mins*　　🍽 **Serves:** *8*

Directions

1. Put the cucumber slices and salt into a strainer and merge to incorporate.
2. Lay out the strainer over a bowl and let it sit for 15-30 minutes.
3. Place the cucumbers into a large-sized bowl.
4. Put in remnant ingredients and merge to incorporate.
5. Shift into your refrigerator to chill before enjoying.

Ingredients

One and half lb. Turkish cucumbers, thinly slivered - Half tsp. kosher salt - Quarter C. red onion, very finely slivered - Half C. fresh dill, cut up - Half C. fresh mint, cut up - Three quarters C. fat-free plain - Greek yogurt - Half C. reduced-fat sour cream - Two tbsp. fresh lemon juice - Two cloves garlic, finely cut up - Cracked black pepper - Half tsp. honey - One tbsp. olive oil

NUTRITIONAL VALUES : TOTAL CALORIES: 104; TOTAL CARBOHYDRATES: 15.2G; DIETARY FIBER: 1.5G; SUGARS: 7.5G; PROTEIN: 2.8G; TOTAL FAT: 5.1G; SATURATED FAT: 1.4G

Garlic Sautéed Spinach
With Pine Nuts

🕐 **Prep:** *10 mins*　　🍽 **Cook:** *5 mins*　　🍽 **Serves:** *4*

Directions

1. Sizzle oil into a large-sized wok on burner at moderate heat.
2. Cook the garlic for around 1 minute.
3. Put in spinach and cook for around 3-4 minutes.
4. Blend in remnant ingredients and enjoy right away.

Ingredients

Two tbsp. olive oil - Two tsp. garlic, finely cut up - One and half lb. fresh spinach - One tsp. lemon zest - Three tbsp. fresh lemon juice - Quarter C. pine nuts, toasted - Salt and powdered black pepper, as desired

NUTRITIONAL VALUES : TOTAL CALORIES: 161; TOTAL CARBOHYDRATES: 8.1G; DIETARY FIBER: 4.2G; SUGARS: 1.3G; PROTEIN: 6.2G; TOTAL FAT: 13.6G; SATURATED FAT: 1.6G

Honey Roasted Carrots
With Fresh Thyme

🕐 **Prep:** *15 mins*　　🍽 **Cook:** *1 hr*　　🍽 **Serves:** *8*

Directions

1. For preheating: set your oven at 350ºF.
2. Put the butter into a Dutch oven and lay out into the oven to melt it.
3. Take off the Dutch oven from oven and merge in the carrots.
4. Put in the honey, thyme, salt and pepper and merge to incorporate.
5. Dust the carrots with brown sugar and bake in your oven for around 55-60 minutes.
6. Take off the cooking pot from oven.
7. With a frying ladle, shift the carrots onto a platter.
8. With a piece of heavy-duty foil, cover the carrots.
9. Place the Dutch oven with any remnant honey sauce on burner at around moderate-high heat.
10. Cook the mixture until boiling.
11. Cook for around 5 minutes, mixing from from time to time.
12. Take off the cooking pot of honey sauce from burner.
13. Ladle the honey sauce over carrots and merge to incorporate.
14. Enjoy right away.

Ingredients

Half C. unsalted butter - Two lb. carrots, peel removed and slivered - One C. honey - One tbsp. fresh thyme, cut up - Salt and powdered black pepper, as desired

NUTRITIONAL VALUES : TOTAL CALORIES: 295; TOTAL CARBOHYDRATES: 50.5G; DIETARY FIBER: 3G; SUGARS: 44.8G; PROTEIN: 1.2G; TOTAL FAT: 11.5G; SATURATED FAT: 7.3G

Tangy Coleslaw
With Apple Cider Vinaigrette

🕐 **Prep:** *15 mins*　　　🍽 **Serves:** *8*

Directions

1. Put the cabbage, carrot and scallion into a large-sized bowl and merge to incorporate thoroughly.
2. Put the vinegar, olive oil, mustard and honey into a small-sized bowl and whisk to incorporate thoroughly.
3. Place the dressing over the cabbage mixture and merge to incorporate thoroughly.
4. Shift into your refrigerator to chill before enjoying.

Ingredients

For the Coleslaw:
Half green cabbage head, shredded - Half head, shredded - Two large-sized carrots, peel removed and shredded - Three scallions, thinly slivered
For the Dressing:
Quarter C. apple cider vinegar - Quarter C. olive oil - One tbsp. grainy or Dijon mustard - Two tbsp. runny honey - Salt and pepper, as desired

NUTRITIONAL VALUES : TOTAL CALORIES: 131; TOTAL CARBOHYDRATES: 16G; DIETARY FIBER: 4G; SUGARS: 11G; PROTEIN: 2G; TOTAL FAT: 8G; SATURATED FAT: 2.1G

Oven-Baked Beet
Chips with Sea Salt

🕐 **Prep:** *10 mins*　　🍲 **Cook:** *30 mins*　　🍽 **Serves:** *4*

Directions

1. For preheating: set your oven at 350°F.
2. Lay out bakery paper onto a large-sized, rimmed baking tray..
3. Put beet slices and oil into a bowl and merge to incorporate.
4. Lay out the beet slices onto the baking tray.
5. Bake in your oven for around 20-30 minutes.

Ingredients

Two small-sized beets, peel removed and slivered thinly - One tbsp. olive oil - Sea salt, as desired

NUTRITIONAL VALUES : TOTAL CALORIES: 52; TOTAL CARBOHYDRATES: 5G; DIETARY FIBER: 1G; SUGARS: 4G; PROTEIN: 0.8G; TOTAL FAT: 3.6G; SATURATED FAT: 1.2G

Mediterranean Orzo Salad
With Feta & Olives

🕐 **Prep:** *15 mins*   🍲 **Cook:** *10 mins*   🍽 **Serves:** *4*

Directions

1. For the salad: cook the orzo into a large-sized cooking pot of salted boiling water for around 8-10 minutes.
2. Drain the orzo and rinse under cold running water.
3. Put pasta and remnant ingredients into a large-sized salad bowl and merge to incorporate.
4. For the dressing: put oil and remnant ingredients into a small-sized bowl and whisk to incorporate thoroughly.
5. Place the dressing over salad and merge to incorporate.
6. Shift into your refrigerator to chill thoroughly before enjoying.

Ingredients

For the Salad:
Half C. uncooked whole-wheat orzo pasta - Three plum tomatoes, cut up - One C. black olives, pitted and slivered - Six C. fresh spinach, roughly cut up - Three scallions, cut up - Half C. feta cheese, crumbled - One tbsp. capers, drained
For the Dressing:
One third C. olive oil - Four tsp. fresh lemon juice One tbsp. fresh parsley, finely cut up - Two tsp. fresh lemon zest, grated - Salt and powdered black pepper, as desired

NUTRITIONAL VALUES : TOTAL CALORIES: 340; TOTAL CARBOHYDRATES: 25.2G; DIETARY FIBER: 4.4G; SUGARS: 4.1G; PROTEIN: 7.9G; TOTAL FAT: 25.1G; SATURATED FAT: 10.8G

Caramelized
Onion and Swiss Chard

🕐 **Prep:** *15 mins*   🍲 **Cook:** *15 mins*   🍽 **Serves:** *4*

Directions

1. Sizzle oil into a cast-iron wok on burner at moderate-high heat.
2. Cook the onions for around 4-5 minutes.
3. Blend in Erythritol and cook for around 2-3 minutes.
4. Blend in chard and olives and cook for around 2-3 minutes.
5. Blend in capers and salt and cook for around 2-3 minutes.
6. Blend in lemon juice, salt and pepper and take off from burner.
7. Enjoy right away.

Ingredients

One large-sized yellow onion, cut up - Two tbsp. olive oil - One tsp. Erythritol - 1 bunch red Swiss chard, cut up - Quarter C. kalamata olives - Two tbsp. capers - Half tsp. sea salt - Powdered black pepper, as desired - 2 tbsp. lemon juice

NUTRITIONAL VALUES : TOTAL CALORIES: 118; TOTAL CARBOHYDRATES: 9G; DIETARY FIBER: 2G; SUGARS: 4G; PROTEIN: 2G; TOTAL FAT: 9G; SATURATED FAT: 1G

Mashed Cauliflower
With Parmesan & Chives

🕐 **Prep:** *10 mins*   📠 **Cook:** *12 mins*   🍽 **Serves:** *4*

Directions

1. Put the cauliflower into a large-sized cooking pot of boiling water and immediately cover it.
2. Cook for around 10-12 minutes.
3. Drain the cauliflower well.
4. In a large-sized food mixer, place the cauliflower, cream, half C. of cheese, butter and pepper and whirl to form a perfectly silky mixture.
5. Shift the cauliflower mash into a bowl.
6. Top with the remnant cheese and parsley and enjoy right away.

Ingredients

One large-sized head cauliflower, cut into florets - One third C. reduced-fat heavy cream - One C. reduced-fat Parmesan cheese, shredded and divided - One tbsp. butter - Powdered black pepper, as desired - One tbsp. fresh parsley, cut up

NUTRITIONAL VALUES : TOTAL CALORIES: 107; TOTAL CARBOHYDRATES: 3G; DIETARY FIBER: 1.1G; SUGARS: 1.1G; PROTEIN: 6.1G; TOTAL FAT: 8.1G; SATURATED FAT: 1.9G

Buttery Herb
Grilled Corn on the Cob

🕐 **Prep:** *10 mins*   📠 **Cook:** *8 mins*   🍽 **Serves:** *6*

Directions

1. Put the basil, parsley, garlic, lemon zest, salt and pepper into the food mixer and whirl to incorporate.
2. Put in butter and whirl to incorporate.
3. Place the butter mixture onto a piece of cling wrap and shape it into a log.
4. Shift into your refrigerator until ready to use.
5. For preheating: set your grill to moderate-high heat.
6. Lightly spray the grill grates.
7. Grill the corn for around 4 minutes from both sides.
8. Take off the corn from grill and place onto a platter.
9. Rub each ear with butter mixture and enjoy right away.

Ingredients

Half C. fresh basil leaves, cut up - Half C. fresh parsley leaves, cut up - Eight cloves garlic - Zest of 1 lemon - One pinch of salt - Powdered black pepper, as desired - Half C. butter, softened - 6 ears corn, shucked and silks cleaned

NUTRITIONAL VALUES : TOTAL CALORIES: 389; TOTAL CARBOHYDRATES: 22G; DIETARY FIBER: 3G; SUGARS: 7G; PROTEIN: 4G; TOTAL FAT: 34G; SATURATED FAT: 20G

Oven-Baked Zucchini
Fries with Garlic Aioli

🕐 **Prep:** *15 mins* 　 📟 **Cook:** *25 mins* 　 🍽 **Serves:** *4*

Directions

1. For the garlic aioli, put mayonnaise and remnant ingredients into a small-sized bowl and merge thoroughly.
2. Cover the bowl and shift into your refrigerator for 20-30 minutes.
3. In a large-sized colander, place zucchini sticks and sprinkle with salt.
4. Put to one side for around 1 hour to drain.
5. For preheating: set your oven at 425°F.
6. Lay out bakery paper onto a large-sized, rimmed baking tray.
7. Squeeze the zucchini sticks to remove excess liquid.
8. With a paper towel, pat dry the zucchini sticks.
9. Whisk the eggs into a shallow dish.
10. Put the remnant ingredients into a second shallow dish and merge thoroughly.
11. Dip the zucchini sticks in egg and then coat with the cheese mixture.
12. Lay out the zucchini sticks onto the baking tray.
13. Bake in your oven for around 25 minutes, turning once halfway through.
14. Enjoy alongside the aioli.

Ingredients

For the Aioli:
Quarter C. mayonnaise - Quarter C. fat-free plain Greek yogurt - Two small-sized cloves garlic, finely cut up - Three quarters tbsp. lemon juice - Quarter tsp. sea salt - Quarter tsp. powdered black pepper

For the Fries:
Two zucchinis, cut into 3-inch sticks lengthwise - Salt, as desired - Two eggs - Half C. Parmesan cheese, grated - Half C. almonds, finely ground - Half tsp. Italian herb easoning

NUTRITIONAL VALUES : TOTAL CALORIES: 218; TOTAL CARBOHYDRATES: 10.8G; DIETARY FIBER: 2.6G; SUGARS: 4.6G; PROTEIN: 11.5G; TOTAL FAT: 15.7G; SATURATED FAT: 3.1G

Citrus Kale Salad
With Toasted Almonds

🕐 **Prep:** *15 mins* 　 🍽 **Serves:** *2*

Directions

1. For salad: put kale and remnant ingredients into a salad bowl and merge to incorporate.
2. For the dressing: place oil and remnant ingredients in another bowl and whisk to incorporate thoroughly.
3. Place dressing on top of salad and merge to incorporate.
4. Enjoy right away.

Ingredients

For the Salad:
Three C. fresh kale, tough ribs removed and torn - Two oranges, peel removed and segmented - Two tbsp. unsweetened dried cranberries - Two tbsp. almonds, toasted and cut up

For the Dressing:
Two tbsp. olive oil - Two tbsp. fresh orange juice - One tsp. Dijon mustard - Half tsp. honey - Salt and powdered black pepper, as desired

NUTRITIONAL VALUES : TOTAL CALORIES: 256; TOTAL CARBOHYDRATES: 31.3G; DIETARY FIBER: 4.8G; SUGARS: 16.6G; PROTEIN: 4.6G; TOTAL FAT: 14.5G; SATURATED FAT: 2.1G

Roasted Brussels Sprouts
With Pecans & Cranberries

🕐 **Prep:** *15 mins*　　🍲 **Cook:** *25 mins*　　🍽 **Serves:** *4*

Directions

1. For preheating: set your oven at 425°F.
2. Lay out bakery paper onto a large-sized, rimmed baking tray.
3. Put the sprouts, oil and salt onto baking tray and merge to incorporate.
4. Roast the sprouts for around 25 minutes.
5. After 20 minutes of cooking, place the pecans onto the baling tray alongside the sprouts.
6. Shift the roasted Brussels sprouts and toasted pecans to a serving platter with cranberries and merge.
7. Drizzle the balsamic vinegar on top.
8. Sprinkle with Parmesan, salt and pepper and enjoy right away.

Ingredients

One and half lb. Brussels sprouts, trimmed and halved - Two tbsp. olive oil - Quarter tsp. fine sea salt - One third C. dried cranberries - One third C. pecans, roughly cut up - One tbsp. balsamic vinegar - One third C. Parmesan cheese, grated - Salt and powdered black pepper, as desired

NUTRITIONAL VALUES : TOTAL CALORIES: 262; TOTAL CARBOHYDRATES: 28.3G; DIETARY FIBER: 8G; SUGARS: 14.4G; PROTEIN: 9.1G; TOTAL FAT: 15.4G; SATURATED FAT: 2.8G

Cold Sesame Cucumber
Noodle Salad

🕐 **Prep:** *15 mins*　　🍽 **Serves:** *2*

Directions

1. Put cucumbers and remnant ingredients into a large-sized bowl and merge to incorporate.
2. Enjoy right away.

Ingredients

2 cucumbers, spiralized wit blade C - One tsp. salt - Two tbsp. sesame oil - Two tbsp. rice vinegar - Two tbsp. sesame seeds

NUTRITIONAL VALUES : TOTAL CALORIES: 107; TOTAL CARBOHYDRATES: 4G; DIETARY FIBER: 1G; SUGARS: 2G; PROTEIN: 1G; TOTAL FAT: 9G; SATURATED FAT: 1.2G

Fluffy Garlic & Herb
Whole-Wheat Couscous

🕐 **Prep:** *10 mins*   📷 **Cook:** *5 mins*   🍽 **Serves:** *6*

Directions

1. In a small-sized cooking pot, put the broth and cumin on burner at moderate-high heat and cook until boiling.
2. Blend in the couscous and immediately take off from burner.
3. Cover the cooking pot and put to one side for around 5 minutes.
4. Takeoff the cover of cooking pot and fluff the couscous with a fork.
5. Shift the couscous into a bowl.
6. Put in remnant ingredients and gently blend to incorporate.
7. Enjoy right away.

Ingredients

One and half C. vegetable broth - One tsp. powdered cumin - One and half C. uncooked couscous - Two cloves garlic, finely cut up - Two tbsp. fresh parsley, cut up - Two tbsp. fresh mint leaves, cut up - Two tsp. fresh orange zest, grated - Three-four tbsp. fresh orange juice - One tbsp. olive oil

NUTRITIONAL VALUES : TOTAL CALORIES: 155; TOTAL CARBOHYDRATES: 16.6G; DIETARY FIBER: 1.2G; SUGARS: 2.4G; PROTEIN: 9.4G; TOTAL FAT: 6G; SATURATED FAT: 1.2G

Charred Broccoli with Chili
& Lemon Zest

🕐 **Prep:** *10 mins*   📷 **Cook:** *25 mins*   🍽 **Serves:** *4*

Directions

1. For preheating: set your oven at 425ºF.
2. Lay out bakery paper onto a baking tray.
3. Put broccoli, oil and salt into a large-sized bowl and merge to incorporate.
4. Spread the cauliflower onto the baking tray.
5. Roast for around 25 minutes, flipping once after 15 minutes.
6. Enjoy right away.

Ingredients

Two large-sized heads broccoli, cut into florets - Three tbsp. olive oil - Kosher salt, as desired

NUTRITIONAL VALUES : TOTAL CALORIES: 129; TOTAL CARBOHYDRATES: 7.6G; DIETARY FIBER: 3G; SUGARS: 1.9G; PROTEIN: 3.2G; TOTAL FAT: 10.9G; SATURATED FAT: 1.5G

Zesty Lime and Shrimp
Skewers

🕐 **Prep:** *15 mins*   🍲 **Cook:** *8 mins*   🍽 **Serves:** *6*

Directions

1. Put oil and remnant ingredients except the shrimp into a large-sized bowl and merge thoroughly.
2. Put in shrimp and coat with the herb mixture.
3. Shift into your refrigerator to marinate for around 30 minutes.
4. For preheating: set your grill to moderate-high heat.
5. Spray the grill grate.
6. Thread the shrimp onto the re soaked wooden skewers.
7. Place the skewers onto the grill and cook for around 3-4 minutes from both sides.
8. Take off the skewers from grill and place onto a platter for around 5 minutes before enjoying.

Ingredients

Quarter C. olive oil - Two tbsp. fresh lime juice - Half chipotle pepper in adobo sauce, seeded and finely cut up - One cloves garlic, finely cut up - One and half tsp. powdered Erythritol - Half tsp. red chili powder - Half tsp. paprika - Quarter tsp. powdered cumin - Salt and powdered black pepper, as desired - Two lb. medium raw shrimp, peel removed and deveined

NUTRITIONAL VALUES : TOTAL CALORIES: 254; TOTAL CARBOHYDRATES: 2.7G; DIETARY FIBER: 0.2G; SUGARS: 0.1G; PROTEIN: 34.5G; TOTAL FAT: 11G; SATURATED FAT: 2G

Classic Deviled Eggs
With a Twist

🕐 **Prep:** *15 mins*   🍲 **Cook:** *5 mins*   🍽 **Serves:** *6*

Directions

1. Put the eggs into a large-sized cooking pot of water on burner at high heat.
2. Cook the water until boiling.
3. Immediately cover the cooking pot of eggs and take off from burner.
4. Put to one side with the cover for around 10-15 minutes.
5. Drain the eggs and let them cool thoroughly.
6. Peel the eggs and, with a sharp knife, slice them in half vertically.
7. Take off the yolks from egg halves.
8. Put half of the egg yolks, avocado, lime juice and salt into a bowl and with a fork, mash to incorporate thoroughly.
9. Scoop the avocado mixture into the egg halves.
10. Enjoy with a sprinkling of cayenne powder.

Ingredients

Six large-sized eggs - One medium-sized avocado, peel removed, pitted and cut up - Two tsp. fresh lime juice - Sea salt, as desired - One pinch of cayenne powder

NUTRITIONAL VALUES : TOTAL CALORIES: 140; TOTAL CARBOHYDRATES: 3.3G; DIETARY FIBER: 2.3G; SUGARS: 0.6G; PROTEIN: 9.6G; TOTAL FAT: 11.5G; SATURATED FAT: 2.6G

Carrot Sticks
With Pesto

🕐 **Prep:** *15 mins*   🍲 **Cook:** *25 mins*   🍽 **Serves:** *8*

Directions

1. For preheating: set your oven at 400°F.
2. Lightly spray 2 large-sized baking trays with oil mist.
3. Divide the carrot sticks onto the baking trays and arrange.
4. Spray the carrot sticks with the oil mist.
5. Roast for around 19-20 minutes.
6. In the meantime, for pesto: put garlic and remnant ingredients except for oil in a clean food mixer and whirl to form a perfectly silky mixture.
7. While the motor is running, slowly, put the oil and whirl to form a perfectly silky mixture.
8. Take off the carrot sticks from oven and merge with pesto.
9. Roast for around 4-5 minutes more.
10. Take off the baking trays of carrot sticks from oven and put to one side to cool slightly.
11. Enjoy moderately hot.

Ingredients

For the Carrot Sticks:
Olive oil mist - Six large-sized carrots, peel removed and cut into 2-inch long sticks
For the Pesto:
One clove garlic, cut up - Half of jalapeño pepper, roughly cut up - Half C. fresh basil, cut up - Half tbsp. fresh lime juice - Half tsp. powdered cumin - One pinch of salt - Powdered black pepper, as desired - Two tbsp. olive oil

NUTRITIONAL VALUES : TOTAL CALORIES: 54; TOTAL CARBOHYDRATES: 5.6G; DIETARY FIBER: 1.4G; SUGARS: 2.7G; PROTEIN: 0.5G; TOTAL FAT: 3.6G; SATURATED FAT: 0.1G

Tomato Bruschetta with Fresh Basil
&Balsamic Reduction

🕐 **Prep:** *15 mins*   🍲 **Cook:** *5 mins*   🍽 **Serves:** *6*

Directions

1. For preheating: set your oven at broiler.
2. Lay out a rack in the top portion of oven.
3. Lay out the bread slices onto a baking tray.
4. Broil for around 2 minutes from both sides.
5. In the meantime, for the balsamic glaze: in a small-sized pot, put the vinegar to a boil on burner at moderate heat.
6. Cook for around 4-5 minutes.
7. Immediately, pour the glaze into a small-sized bowl and put to one side to cool.
8. Put tomatoes and remnant ingredients into a bowl and merge to incorporate.
9. Place the tomato mixture on each toasted bread slice and drizzle with balsamic reduction.
10. Enjoy right away.

Ingredients

Half of whole-grain baguette, cut into six (half-inch-thick) slices - One third C. balsamic vinegar - Three tomatoes, cut up - Half C. fennel, cut up - Two cloves garlic, finely cut up - One tbsp. fresh parsley, cut up - One tbsp. fresh basil, cut up - Two tsp. fresh lemon juice - One tsp. olive oil - Salt and powdered black pepper, as desired

NUTRITIONAL VALUES : TOTAL CALORIES: 102; TOTAL CARBOHYDRATES: 16.3G; DIETARY FIBER: 3G; SUGARS: 3.7G; PROTEIN: 3.7G; TOTAL FAT: 2.4G; SATURATED FAT: 0.1G

Spinach & Feta
Stuffed Mushrooms

🕐 **Prep:** *15 mins*   📟 **Cook:** *23 mins*   🍽 **Serves:** *6*

Directions

1. For preheating: set your oven at 400ºF.
2. Sizzle the oil into a wok on burnet at moderate heat.
3. Add spinach and sauté for around 1 minute.
4. Put in garlic and cook for around 1 minute.
5. Take off from burner.
6. Put the spinach and feta cheese into a small-sized bowl and merge.
7. Fill each mushroom with spinach mixture.
8. Lay out the mushrooms onto a baking tray.
9. Bake in your oven for around 20 minutes.
10. Enjoy moderately hot or cold.

Ingredients

One tbsp. olive oil - Two C. fresh spinach - Three and half oz. reduced-fat feta cheese - One clove garlic - Twelve button mushrooms

NUTRITIONAL VALUES : TOTAL CALORIES: 37; TOTAL CARBOHYDRATES: 1G; DIETARY FIBER: 0G; SUGARS: 1G; PROTEIN: 2G; TOTAL FAT: 3G; SATURATED FAT: 1G

Mini Turkey
Lettuce Wraps

🕐 **Prep:** *15 mins*   📟 **Cook:** *15 mins*   🍽 **Serves:** *6*

Directions

1. Sizzle oil into a deep wok on burner at moderate heat.
2. Cook the onions for around 5 minutes.
3. Put in ground turkey and cook for around 6-7 minutes.
4. Blend in the garlic, bell pepper and spices and cook for around 1-2 minutes.
5. Place turkey mixture over each lettuce leaf and
6. Top with avocado and enjoy right away.
7. Lettuce wraps with turkey

Ingredients

One tbsp. olive oil - One medium-sized yellow onion diced - One lb. ground turkey - One large-sized bell pepper, seeded and cut up - One clove garlic - One tbsp. chili powder - One tsp. salt - One tsp. powdered black pepper - One large-sized avocado, peeled, pitted and cut up - Six lettuce leaves

NUTRITIONAL VALUES : TOTAL CALORIES: 248; TOTAL CARBOHYDRATES: 5.6G; DIETARY FIBER: 3.1G; SUGARS: 1.3G; PROTEIN: 20G; TOTAL FAT: 17.4G; SATURATED FAT: 3.1G

Crispy Baked Cauliflower Bites
With Garlic Yogurt Dip

🕐 **Prep:** *20 mins*　　📠 **Cook:** *30 mins*　　🍽 **Serves:** *4*

Directions

1. For preheating: set your oven at 350ºF.
2. For the cauliflower: put cauliflower and remnant ingredients into a large-sized bowl and merge to incorporate.
3. Lay out the cauliflower florets onto a baking tray.
4. Bake in your oven for around 20 minutes.
5. Take off the baking tray of cauliflower from oven and coat the cauliflower with peri peri sauce.
6. Bake in your oven for around 9-10 minutes.
7. In the meantime, for the dip, put all ingredients into a bowl and merge to incorporate.
8. Enjoy cauliflower bites alongside the dip.

Ingredients

For the Cauliflower Bites:
One cauliflower head, broken into small-sized florets - One tsp. garlic powder - Two tsp. paprika - Half tsp. chili powder - Two tsp. olive oil - 4 tbsp. sugar-free peri peri sauce
For the Dip:
Twelve oz. fat-free plain Greek yogurt - Salt, as desired - One tsp. garlic powder - Half tsp. lime juice

NUTRITIONAL VALUES : TOTAL CALORIES: 97; TOTAL CARBOHYDRATES: 10.1G; DIETARY FIBER: 2.1G; SUGARS: 7.3G; PROTEIN: 5.9G; TOTAL FAT: 3.5G; SATURATED FAT: 1.1G

Roasted Red
Pepper & Walnut Dip

🕐 **Prep:** *15 mins*　　📠 **Cook:** *15 mins*　　🍽 **Serves:** *6*

Directions

1. For preheating: set your oven at 350ºF.
2. Place the bell pepper over the open flame of a gas burner.
3. Cook for around 15 minutes.
4. Put the blackened peppers into a bowl and immediately cover with cling wrap.
5. Put to one side to steam.
6. Peel the red peppers and discard the seeds.
7. Put peppers and remnant ingredients into the food mixer and whirl to form a perfectly silky mixture.
8. The sauce is ready to use.

Ingredients

Two red bell peppers - One and half C. r walnuts, toasted and cut up - Three cloves garlic, cut up - Two tsp. paprika - One tsp. powdered cumin - One tsp. red pepper flakes - Quarter C. fresh lemon juice - Two and half tbsp. maple syrup - Two tbsp. olive oil - Kosher salt and powdered black pepper

NUTRITIONAL VALUES : TOTAL CALORIES: 424; TOTAL CARBOHYDRATES: 23G; DIETARY FIBER: 5G; SUGARS: 14G; PROTEIN: 8G; TOTAL FAT: 37G; SATURATED FAT: 4G

Tuna
Croquettes

🕐 **Prep:** *15 mins*   ▣ **Cook:** *31 mins*   🍽 **Serves:** *12*

Directions

1. Put the tuna, mayonnaise, eggs, onion, scallion, garlic, almond flour, salt and pepper into a large-sized bowl and merge to incorporate thoroughly.
2. Shape the mixture in 8 oblong patties.
3. Sizzle the oil into a large-sized wok on burner at moderate-high heat.
4. Cook the croquettes in 2 batches for around 2-4 minutes from both sides.
5. With a frying ladle, shift the croquettes onto a plate lined with paper towels.
6. Enjoy moderately hot.

Ingredients

Twenty four oz. canned white tuna, drained - Quarter C. mayonnaise - Four large-sized eggs - Two tbsp. yellow onion, finely cut up - One scallion, slivered thinly - Four cloves garlic, finely cut up - Three quarters C. almond flour - Salt and powdered black pepper, as desired - Quarter C. olive oil

NUTRITIONAL VALUES : TOTAL CALORIES: 311; TOTAL CARBOHYDRATES: 17G; DIETARY FIBER: 3G; SUGARS: 11G; PROTEIN: 32G; TOTAL FAT: 14G; SATURATED FAT: 3G

Spiced Chicken Satay
With Peanut Dipping Sauce

🕐 **Prep:** *20 mins*   ▣ **Cook:** *18 mins*   🍽 **Serves:** *4*

Directions

1. For the chicken: put chicken strips and remnant ingredients into a large-sized bowl and merge to incorporate.
2. With cling wrap, cover the bowl of chicken and shift into your refrigerator overnight.
3. Take off the bowl of chicken from refrigerator and put it aside at room temperature for 30 minutes before grilling.
4. In the meantime, for the peanut sauce: put the broth, peanut butter, honey, soy sauce, fish sauce, Sriracha, ginger and garlic into a medium-sized cooking pot on burner at moderate heat.
5. Cook the mixture until boiling.
6. Cook for around 6 minutes.
7. Blend in the lime juice and take off from burner. Put it to one side.
8. For preheating: set your outdoor grill to moderate-high heat.
9. Thread the chicken onto skewers.
10. Grill the chicken skewers for around 2-3 minutes from both sides.
11. Enjoy moderately hot with sauce.

Ingredients

For the Chicken:
One lb. boneless chicken breasts, cut into 1-inch strips - Two tbsp. reduced-sodium soy sauce - Half tbsp. fish sauce - Two tbsp. fresh lime juice - One tbsp. honey - One tbsp. Sriracha sauce - Two tsp. powdered ginger - Two cloves garlic finely cut up
For the Peanut Sauce:
One C. chicken broth - 5 tbsp. creamy peanut butter - One tbsp. honey - One tbsp. reduced-sodium soy sauce - Two tsp. fish sauce - Two tsp. Sriracha - One tsp. powdered ginger - Two cloves garlic, finely cut up - One tbsp. fresh lime juice

NUTRITIONAL VALUES : TOTAL CALORIES: 311; TOTAL CARBOHYDRATES: 17G; DIETARY FIBER: 3G; SUGARS: 11G; PROTEIN: 32G; TOTAL FAT: 14G; SATURATED FAT: 3G

Guacamole & Salsa Stuffed
Mini Bell Peppers

🕐 **Prep:** *15 mins*   📷 **Cook:** *4 mins*   🔔 **Serves:** *15*

Directions

1. Lay out the rack 4-inch from t heating element.
2. For preheating: set your oven to broiler.
3. Put avocados, beans, corn and salsa into a bowl and merge to incorporate.
4. Stuff each pepper with mixture.
5. Lay out the peppers onto the baking tray.
6. Top each pepper with cheese.
7. Broil for around 2-4 minutes.
8. Enjoy moderately hot.

Ingredients

One avocado, peeled, pitted and finely cut up - Three quarters C. canned black beans, rinsed - Half C. frozen corn, thawed - Half C. chunky mild salsa - Fifteen assorted mini sweet peppers, halved lengthwise and seeded - One C. reduced-fat cheddar cheese, shredded

NUTRITIONAL VALUES : TOTAL CALORIES: 80; TOTAL CARBOHYDRATES: 8G; DIETARY FIBER: 3G; SUGARS: 2G; PROTEIN: 3G; TOTAL FAT: 4.5G; SATURATED FAT: 1.5G

Low-Carb Cheesy
Zucchini Fritters

🕐 **Prep:** *20 mins*   📷 **Cook:** *20 mins*   🔔 **Serves:** *12*

Directions

1. Put the shredded zucchini and salt into a large-sized bowl and merge to incorporate.
2. Put it to one side for around 9-10 minutes.
3. For preheating: set your oven at 400ºF.
4. Lay out bakery paper onto two large-sized baking trays and then spray each with oil mist.
5. Squeeze the zucchini to drain water.
6. Put zucchini and remnant ingredients into a large-sized bowl and merge to incorporate.
7. Scoop batter onto baking trays and with your hands, press each slightly.
8. Spray top with oil mist.
9. Bake in your oven for around 20 minutes, flipping once halfway through.
10. Enjoy moderately hot.

Ingredients

Three medium-sized zucchini, shredded - One tsp. salt - Two large-sized eggs - Quarter C. reduced-fat feta cheese, crumbled - Quarter C. part-skim mozzarella cheese, shredded - Two cloves garlic, finely cut up - Two scallions, finely cut up - Quarter C. fresh parsley, finely cut up - Salt and powdered black pepper, as desired - Half C. almond flour - One tbsp. olive oil

NUTRITIONAL VALUES : TOTAL CALORIES: 76; TOTAL CARBOHYDRATES: 3G; DIETARY FIBER: 1G; SUGARS: 2G; PROTEIN: 4G; TOTAL FAT: 6G; SATURATED FAT: 1G

Tuna & Avocado
Stuffed Cherry Tomatoes

🕐 **Prep:** *15 mins*   🍽 **Serves:** *8*

Directions

1. Carefully scoop out the seeds and pulp from each tomato.
2. Put remnant ingredients into a bowl and merge thoroughly.
3. Stuff each tomato with mixture and enjoy right away.

Ingredients

Two C. cherry tomatoes - One (six-oz.) can tuna fish - Three tbsp. mayonnaise - One tbsp. relish - Half tsp. garlic powder - One tsp. dried onion

NUTRITIONAL VALUES : TOTAL CALORIES: 56; TOTAL CARBOHYDRATES: 3.7G; DIETARY FIBER: 0.5G; SUGARS: 2G; PROTEIN: 20G; TOTAL FAT: 15G; SATURATED FAT: 5G

Rosemary & Lemon
Grilled Chicken Wings

🕐 **Prep:** *15 mins*   📱 **Cook:** *20 mins*   🍽 **Serves:** *8*

Directions

1. Put the chicken wings and remnant ingredients except for parsley into a large-sized resealable storage bag.
2. Seal the bag of chicken wings tightly and shake vigorously to coat well.
3. Shift the bag of wings into your refrigerator for around 1 hour.
4. For preheating: set your grill to moderate heat.
5. Lightly spray the grill grate with oil mist.
6. Lay out the chicken wings onto the grill.
7. Cook for around 18-20 minutes.
8. Enjoy right away.

Ingredients

Three lb. chicken wings - Six tbsp. olive oil - Three tbsp. balsamic vinegar - Five cloves garlic, finely cut up - One tbsp. dried rosemary - One and half tsp. kosher salt - One and half tsp. powdered black pepper - Two tbsp. fresh parsley, finely cut up

NUTRITIONAL VALUES : TOTAL CALORIES: 335; TOTAL CARBOHYDRATES: 3.4G; DIETARY FIBER: G; SUGARS: 1.2G; PROTEIN: 28.5G; TOTAL FAT: 24.6G; SATURATED FAT: 6.8G

Coconut Shrimp

🕐 **Prep:** *20 mins*   📟 **Cook:** *20 mins*   🍽 **Serves:** *8*

Directions

1. For preheating: set your oven at 425°F.
2. Lay out bakery paper onto a large-sized baking tray.
3. Whisk the eggs into a shallow dish.
4. Put the remnant ingredients except for coconut and shrimp into a second shallow dish and merge thoroughly.
5. Put the coconut flakes into a third shallow dish.
6. Dip the shrimp into whipped eggs and then roll into breadcrumb mixture.
7. Again dip in eggs and then roll into coconut flakes.
8. Lay out the shrimp onto the baking tray.
9. Bake in your oven for around 15-20 minutes.
10. Enjoy moderately hot.

Ingredients

Three eggs - Half C. whole-wheat breadcrumbs - One tsp. garlic powder - One tsp. onion powder - Quarter tsp. cayenne powder - Salt and powdered white pepper, as desired - Half C. unsweetened coconut flakes - Twenty four medium raw shrimp, peeled and deveined

NUTRITIONAL VALUES : TOTAL CALORIES: 176; TOTAL CARBOHYDRATES: 4.7G; DIETARY FIBER: 1.1G; SUGARS: 1.3G; PROTEIN: 18G; TOTAL FAT: 7.2G; SATURATED FAT: 4.5G

Cottage Cheese & Strawberry Bowl

🕐 **Prep:** *10 mins*   🍽 **Serves:** *2*

Directions

1. Put cottage cheese and strawberry slices into a medium-sized bowl and merge them.
2. Enjoy right away.

Ingredients

One third C. reduced-fat cottage cheese
Quarter C. fresh strawberries, hulled and sliced

NUTRITIONAL VALUES : TOTAL CALORIES: 40; TOTAL CARBOHYDRATES: 0.1G; DIETARY FIBER: 0.4G; SUGARS: 1G; PROTEIN: 5.3G; TOTAL FAT: 0.8G; SATURATED FAT: 2.4G

Baked Mozzarella Sticks
With Marinara Dip

🕐 **Prep:** *20 mins*　　🍲 **Cook:** *20 mins*　　🍽 **Serves:** *6*

Directions

1. Put the flour into a shallow dish.
2. Whisk together the eggs and milk in a second shallow dish.
3. Put the breadcrumbs, Italian seasoning, garlic powder, salt and pepper into a third shallow dish and merge thoroughly.
4. Coat the mozzarella sticks in flour and then dip them into egg mixture.
5. Finally coat the mozzarella sticks with the breadcrumb mixture.
6. Lay out the breaded mozzarella sticks onto a cookie tray.
7. Freeze for around 30-40 minutes.
8. Lay out the oven rack onto the center position.
9. For preheating: set your oven at 415°F.
10. Lay out the mozzarella sticks onto te baking tray.
11. Bake in your oven for around 15-20 minutes.
12. For the marinara sauce: sizzle olive oil into a cooking pot on burner at moderate heat.
13. Cook the garlic for around 1 minute.
14. Add crushed tomatoes and cook the mixture until boiling.
15. Put in Italian seasoning, salt and pepper and merge thoroughly.
16. Immediately turn the heat at around low.
17. Cook for around 10-15 minutes, blending from time to time.
18. Enjoy mozzarella sticks with marinara sauce.

Ingredients

For the Mozzarella Sticks:
Twelve pieces mozzarella sticks - Two eggs - Two tbsp. reduced-fat milk - One C. almond flour - Two C. whole-wheat breadcrumbs - One tsp. Italian seasoning - One tsp. garlic powder - Salt and powdered black pepper, as desired

For the Marinara Sauce:
One C. crushed tomatoes - One tbsp. olive oil - Two cloves garlic, finely cut up - Half tsp. Italian seasoning - Salt and powdered black pepper, as desired

NUTRITIONAL VALUES : TOTAL CALORIES: 430; TOTAL CARBOHYDRATES: 32G; DIETARY FIBER: 3G; SUGARS: 4G; PROTEIN: 21G; TOTAL FAT: 8G; SATURATED FAT: 8G

Veggie Latkes

🕐 **Prep:** *15 mins*   📱 **Cook:** *20 mins*   🍽 **Serves:** *8*

Directions

1. For latkes: in a large-sized bowl, mix together arrowroot powder, almond flour, salt and pepper.
2. In the bowl of flour mixture, put remnant ingredients except for oil and merge to incorporate thoroughly.
3. Shape the mixture into 8 patties.
4. Sizzle oil into a large-sized, anti-sticking wok on burner at moderate heat.
5. Cook 2 latkes for around 2-3 minutes.
6. Flip each latke and cook for around 2 minutes more.
7. Cook the remnant latkes in the same manner.
8. Enjoy moderately hot.

Ingredients

Quarter C. arrowroot powder - One C. almond flour - Salt and powdered black pepper, as require - One medium-sized carrot, peel removed and shredded - Two medium-sized zucchinis, shredded - One small-sized red onion, cut up - Two small-sized cloves garlic, finely cut up - One jalapeño pepper, cut up finely - Two eggs, beaten - Two tbsp. olive oil

NUTRITIONAL VALUES : TOTAL CALORIES: 162; TOTAL CARBOHYDRATES: 10.4G; DIETARY FIBER: 2.5G; SUGARS: 1.7G; PROTEIN: 5.2G; TOTAL FAT: 11.4G; SATURATED FAT: 1.4G

Broccoli Tots

🕐 **Prep:** *15 mins*   📱 **Cook:** *35 mins*   🍽 **Serves:** *12*

Directions

1. For preheating: set your oven at 400°F.
2. Line two baking trays with bakery paper and then lightly spray with oil mist.
3. Put the broccoli into a microwave-safe dish and microwave with the cover for around 5 minutes, blending once halfway through.
4. Drain the broccoli well.
5. In a large-sized bowl, place the eggs, oregano, garlic powder, cayenne powder, salt and white pepper and whisk to incorporate thoroughly.
6. Put in cooked broccoli, cheddar cheese and almond flour and merge to incorporate thoroughly.
7. With slightly wet hands, make 24 patties from the mixture.
8. Lay out the patties onto baking trays about 2-inch apart.
9. Lightly, spray each patty with oil mist.
10. Bake in your oven for around 15 minutes from both sides.
11. Take off the baking trays of broccoli tots from oven and enjoy moderately hot.

Ingredients

One (sixteen-oz.) package frozen cut up broccoli - Three large-sized eggs - Half tsp. dried oregano - Half tsp. garlic powder - Quarter tsp. cayenne powder - Salt and ground white pepper, as desired - One C. reduced-fat cheddar cheese, grated - One C. almond flour - Olive oil mist

NUTRITIONAL VALUES : TOTAL CALORIES: 165; TOTAL CARBOHYDRATES: 4.9G; DIETARY FIBER: 2.3G; SUGARS: 1.2G; PROTEIN: 3.2G; TOTAL FAT: 7.5G; SATURATED FAT: 0.8G

Chicken Nuggets

🕐 **Prep:** *15 mins*   🍲 **Cook:** *30 mins*   🍽 **Serves:** *4*

Directions

1. For preheating: set your oven at 350°F.
2. Spray a baking tray.
3. Whisk the eggs into a shallow dish.
4. Put the flour, oregano, spices, salt and pepper in a second shallow dish and merge to incorporate thoroughly.
5. Coat the chicken nuggets with whisked eggs and then roll into flour mixture.
6. Lay out the chicken nuggets onto the baking tray.
7. Bake in your oven for around 30 minutes.
8. Take off the baking tray of nuggets from oven and put it to one side to cool slightly.
9. Enjoy moderately hot.

Ingredients

Two (eight-oz.) boneless chicken breasts, cut into 2x1-inch chunks - Two eggs - One C. almond flour - One tsp. dried oregano - Half tsp. onion powder - Half tsp. garlic powder - Half tsp. paprika - Salt and powdered black pepper, as desired

NUTRITIONAL VALUES : TOTAL CALORIES: 179; TOTAL CARBOHYDRATES: 3G; DIETARY FIBER: 1.7G; SUGARS: 0.7G; PROTEIN: 14.1G; TOTAL FAT: 10.7G; SATURATED FAT: 1.9G

Dark Chocolate
Avocado Mousse

🕐 **Prep:** *10 mins*　　🍽 **Serves:** *6*

Directions

1. Put avocados and remnant ingredients into a mixer and whirl to form a perfectly silky mixture.
2. Shift the mousse in serving glasses.
3. Shift the glasses of mousse into your refrigerator to chill thoroughly.

Ingredients

2 ripe avocados, peel removed, pitted and cut up - Half C. coconut milk - Half C. cacao powder - One tsp. powdered cinnamon - Quarter tsp. powdered ancho chile - One third C. raw honey - Two tsp. vanilla extract

NUTRITIONAL VALUES : TOTAL CALORIES: 246; TOTAL CARBOHYDRATES: 25.6G; DIETARY FIBER: 6.7G; SUGARS: 2.9G; PROTEIN: 2.9G; TOTAL FAT: 17.2G; SATURATED FAT: 6.1G

Berry Bliss
Chia Seed Pudding

🕐 **Prep:** *10 mins*　　🍽 **Serves:** *2*

Directions

1. Put the berries, maple syrup and almond milk into a mixer and whirl to form a perfectly silky mixture.
2. Shift the berries mixture into a bowl and merge in the chia seeds.
3. Shift into your refrigerator for around 2 hours before enjoying.

Ingredients

Half C. fresh berries - One C unsweetened almond milk - One tsp. maple syrup - Three tbsp. chia seeds - One C. fat-free plain Greek yogurt

NUTRITIONAL VALUES : TOTAL CALORIES: 244; TOTAL CARBOHYDRATES: 29.7G; DIETARY FIBER: 8.2G; SUGARS: 14.4G; PROTEIN: 9.6G; TOTAL FAT: 10.1G; SATURATED FAT: 1.1G

Light Vanilla Bean Panna Cotta with Berry Compote

🕐 **Prep:** *20 mins*   🍲 **Cook:** *25 mins*   🍽 **Serves:** *6*

Directions

1. For the panna cotta: put half C. of cream into a medium-sized cooking pot.
2. Sprinkle the top with gelatin and let it sit for around 3 minutes.
3. Add remnant cream and sweetener and merge to incorporate.
4. Split the vanilla bean lengthwise and then scrape out the seeds.
5. Put pods and seeds into the cream mixture.
6. Place the pan of mixture on burner at moderate heat.
7. Cook the mixture until steam rises from the surface, whisking all the time.
8. Take off the pan from burner and remove the vanilla bean pod.
9. Put in milk and vanilla extract and merge thoroughly.
10. Place the mixture into dessert glasses.
11. Cover each with cling wrap and shift into your refrigerator to chill for around 3-4 hours.
12. For the cranberry coulis: put cranberries, water and sweetener into a small-sized cooking pot on burner at moderate heat.
13. Cook the mixture until boiling.
14. Cook for around 7-10 minutes.
15. Stir in orange juice and take off from burner.
16. With a hand-held blender, blend the mixture to form a perfectly silky mixture.
17. Through a fine mesh sieve, strain the berry mixture into a bowl.
18. Top each panna cotta with cranberry coulis and enjoy right away.

Ingredients

For the Panna Cotta:
One and Half C. reduced-fat heavy cream, divided - One tbsp. grass-fed gelatin - Half C. Swerve Sweetener - One C. fat-free milk - 1 vanilla bean - Half tsp. vanilla extract

For the Cranberry Coulis:
One C. fresh cranberries - One C. water - One third C. powdered Swerve sweetener - Two tbsp. orange juice

NUTRITIONAL VALUES : TOTAL CALORIES: 142; TOTAL CARBOHYDRATES: 25.7G; DIETARY FIBER: 1.3G; SUGARS: 23.5G; PROTEIN: 3.3G; TOTAL FAT: 12.1G; SATURATED FAT: 7.4G

Lemon Ricotta
Almond Cake

🕐 **Prep:** *15 mins*   🍲 **Cook:** *45 mins*   🍽 **Serves:** *8*

Directions

1. For preheating: set your oven at 325°F.
2. Spray a 9-inch round spring form pan.
3. Put the butter, ricotta, egg yolks, almond extract, Swerve, stevia and salt into the bowl of an electric mixer and merge to incorporate.
4. Put in almond flour and lemon zest and merge to incorporate.
5. Put egg whites with cream of tartar into a clean, glass bowl and whisk to form stiff peaks.
6. Gently blend the whipped egg whites into the flour mixture.
7. Place the batter into the cake pan and sprinkle with slivered almonds.
8. Bake in your oven for around 40-45 minutes.
9. Take off the cake pan from oven and place it onto the cooling grid for around 9-10 minutes.
10. Carefully turn the cake onto the cooling grid to allow it to reach room temperature before enjoying.
11. Dust with Swerve confectioners and enjoy right away.

Ingredients

Half C. butter, softened - One C. ricotta cheese - Four eggs, separated - One tsp. almond extract - Three quarters C. Swerve confectioners - Half tsp. vanilla stevia - Quarter tsp. salt - Two and half C. blanched almond flour - One tsp. lemon zest - Half tsp. cream of tartar - One third C. slivered almonds - Swerve Confectioners, for dusting

NUTRITIONAL VALUES : TOTAL CALORIES: 341; TOTAL CARBOHYDRATES: 26.3G; DIETARY FIBER: 3.4G; SUGARS: 18.4G; PROTEIN: 11.7G; TOTAL FAT: 29.5G; SATURATED FAT: 12.3G

Spiced
Applesauce Cake

🕐 **Prep:** *15 mins*   🍲 **Cook:** *30 mins*   🍽 **Serves:** *12*

Directions

1. For preheating: set your oven at 375°F.
2. Spray 9x13-inch cake pan with oil mist.
3. Put oil, apple concentrate and egg whites into a bowl and whisk to incorporate.
4. Put in applesauce and vanilla extract and whisk to incorporate.
5. Put flour, oats, baking powder, baking soda and spices into another bowl and merge to incorporate.
6. Put flour mixture into the bowl with oil mixture and merge to incorporate.
7. Place the cake mixture into the cake pan.
8. Bake in your oven for around 25-30 minutes.
9. Take off the cake pan from oven and place it onto the cooling grid for around 9-10 minutes.
10. Carefully turn the cake onto the cooling grid to allow it to reach room temperature.
11. Cut into slices and enjoy right away.

Ingredients

Quarter C. olive oil - One and Half C. frozen unsweetened apple juice concentrate, thawed - Three large-sized egg whites - Half C. unsweetened applesauce - One tsp. vanilla extract - Two and half C. whole-wheat flour - One C. gluten-free quick-cooking rolled oats - Three quarter tsp. baking soda - Two tsp. baking powder - One tsp. powdered cinnamon - Quarter tsp. powdered nutmeg - Quarter tsp. powdered cloves - One C. apple, peel removed, cored and grated

NUTRITIONAL VALUES : TOTAL CALORIES: 251; TOTAL CARBOHYDRATES: 38.6G; DIETARY FIBER: 6.3G; SUGARS: 2.1G; PROTEIN: 8.2G; TOTAL FAT: 8.3G; SATURATED FAT: 1.3G

No-Bake Peanut Butter
Protein Balls

🕐 **Prep:** *15 mins*   🍽 **Serves:** *10*

Directions

1. Put the oats into the food mixer and whirl until powdered.
2. Put in peanut butter, honey, vanilla and cinnamon and whirl until just incorporated.
3. Shift the oat mixture into a bowl and merge in the chocolate chips.
4. Cover the bowl and shift into your refrigerator for around 20 minutes.
5. Make 1-inch balls from the mixture.
6. Enjoy right away.

Ingredients

One C. gluten-free old-fashioned oats - Half C. peanut butter - Three tbsp. honey - One tsp. vanilla extract - Half tsp. powdered cinnamon - Quarter C. unsweetened dark chocolate chips

NUTRITIONAL VALUES : TOTAL CALORIES: 150; TOTAL CARBOHYDRATES: 15.9G; DIETARY FIBER: 1.8G; SUGARS: 8.7G; PROTEIN: 4.7G; TOTAL FAT: 8.3G; SATURATED FAT: 2.3G

Cinnamon Swirl
Baked Donuts

🕐 **Prep:** *20 mins*   📦 **Cook:** *28 mins*   🍽 **Serves:** *6*

Directions

1. For preheating: set your oven at 350ºF.
2. Generously spray the holes of a donut pan.
3. Put the eggs, almond milk, butter and vanilla extract into a large-sized bowl and whisk to incorporate thoroughly.
4. Put the flour, Erythritol, baking powder, cinnamon and salt into a second bowl and merge thoroughly.
5. Put in egg mixture and whisk to incorporate thoroughly.
6. Place the mixture into each donut hole.
7. Bake in your oven for around 22-28 minutes.
8. Take off the donut pan from oven and place onto the cooling grid for around 5-7 minutes.
9. In the meantime, for topping: put the Erythritol and cinnamon into a small-sized bowl and merge thoroughly.
10. Carefully take off the donuts from the holes and place onto a chopping block.
11. Coat each donut first with the butter and then with the cinnamon mixture.
12. Enjoy moderately hot.

Ingredients

For Donuts:
Two large-sized eggs - Quarter C. unsweetened almond milk - Quarter C. coconut oil r, melted (measured solid) - Half tsp. vanilla extract - One C. almond flour - One third C. Erythritol - Two tsp. baking powder - One tsp. powdered cinnamon - One pinch of salt
For Topping:
Half C. Erythritol - One tsp. powdered cinnamon - Three tbsp. coconut oil, melted (measured solid)

NUTRITIONAL VALUES : TOTAL CALORIES: 278; TOTAL CARBOHYDRATES: 5.3G; DIETARY FIBER: 2.3G; SUGARS: 0.2G; PROTEIN: 6.2G; TOTAL FAT: 26.6G; SATURATED FAT: 14.9G

Pumpkin Spiced
Oatmeal Cookies

🕐 **Prep:** *15 mins*　　🍲 **Cook:** *35 mins*　　🍽 **Serves:** *16*

Directions

1. For preheating: set your oven at 350ºF.
2. Line baking tray with bakery paper.
3. Put oats into the food mixer and whirl until roughly cut up.
4. Shift the oats into a bowl and merge with flour, baking powder, spices and salt.
5. In a separate bowl, put pumpkin puree and maple syrup and whisk to incorporate.
6. Place maple mixture into the bowl of flour mixture and merge to incorporate.
7. With a cookie scooper, place the cookies onto the cookie tray about 2-inch apart.
8. With the fingers of your hand, flatten each cookie slightly.
9. Bake in your oven for approximately 30-35 minutes.
10. Take off the cookie tray from oven and place it onto the cooling grid for around 5 minutes.
11. Then invert the cookies onto the cooling grid to allow them to reach room temperature before enjoying.

Ingredients

Three C. gluten-free old-fashioned oats - One C. almond flour - Half tsp. baking powder - Two tsp. powdered cinnamon - One tsp. powdered ginger - One tsp. powdered cloves - Half tsp. salt - One (fifteen-oz.) can sugar-free pumpkin puree - Half C. maple syrup

NUTRITIONAL VALUES : TOTAL CALORIES: 166; TOTAL CARBOHYDRATES: 29.5G; DIETARY FIBER: 3.6G; SUGARS: 8.7G; PROTEIN: 4.4G; TOTAL FAT: 3.4G; SATURATED FAT: 0.8G

Chocolate Dipped Strawberries
With Crushed Almonds

🕐 **Prep:** *15 mins*　　🍽 **Serves:** *4*

Directions

1. Put chocolate into a microwave-safe dish and microwave on high setting for around 1½-2 minutes, blending after every 20 seconds.
2. Place the almonds and salt into a small-sized bowl and then blend them well.
3. Place a toothpick into the stem end of each strawberry.
4. Dip the strawberries into melted chocolate and then coat with almonds.
5. Let the strawberries sit for around 20 minutes before enjoying.

Ingredients

Two oz. unsweetened dark chocolate, cut up - Twelve fresh strawberries - Quarter C. almonds, finely cut up - One pinch of kosher salt

NUTRITIONAL VALUES : TOTAL CALORIES: 126; TOTAL CARBOHYDRATES: 16.8G; DIETARY FIBER: 1.7G; SUGARS: 12.1G; PROTEIN: 1.2G; TOTAL FAT: 7.6G; SATURATED FAT: 3.5G

Orange Zest and Cranberry
Biscotti

🕐 **Prep:** *20 mins*　　🖵 **Cook:** *39 mins*　　🛎 **Serves:** *12*

Directions

1. For preheating: set your oven at 325ºF.
2. Lay out bakery paper onto a baking tray.
3. Put butter and Erythritol into a bowl and whisk to form a creamy mixture.
4. Put in eggs, orange zest and both extracts and whisk to incorporate.
5. Put flour, baking soda, baking powder and salt into a separate bowl and merge to incorporate.
6. Put flour mixture into the bowl with egg mixture and merge to form a stiff dough.
7. Gently blend in the cranberries.
8. Cut the dough into two portions and then shape them into logs.
9. Lay out the logs onto baking tray.
10. Bake in your oven for around 20-25 minutes.
11. Take off from oven and place the baking tray onto the cooling grid for around 5 minutes.
12. Carefully turn the logs onto the cooling grid to allow it to reach room temperature.
13. Again, set your oven at 325ºF.
14. Cut the logs into slices and arrange them onto a large-sized baking tray.
15. Bake in your oven for around 7 minutes.
16. Immediately set your oven at 300ºF.
17. Bake in your oven for around 7 minutes.
18. Take off from oven and place the baking tray onto the cooling grid to allow it to reach room temperature before enjoying.

Ingredients

Half C. butter, softened - One C. Erythritol - Two eggs - One tbsp. orange zest, grated - One tsp. orange extract - Quarter tsp. almond extract - Two and three quarters C. almond flour - One tsp. baking powder - Half tsp. baking soda - Quarter tsp. salt - One (six-oz.) package unsweetened dried cranberries

NUTRITIONAL VALUES : TOTAL CALORIES: 241; TOTAL CARBOHYDRATES: 7.2G; DIETARY FIBER: 3.3G; SUGARS: 0.7G; PROTEIN:6.5; TOTAL FAT: 20.6G; SATURATED FAT: 6G

Banana Bread
With Walnuts & Flaxseed

🕐 **Prep:** *15 mins*   ▣ **Cook:** *55 mins*   🛎 **Serves:** *8*

Directions

1. For preheating: set your oven at 350°F.
2. Spray bread mold with oil mist.
3. Put bananas into a large-sized bowl and with a fork, mash well.
4. Add applesauce, Erythritol, oil and eggs and whisk to incorporate.
5. Put flour, flax, baking soda, allspice, cinnamon and salt into a medium-sized bowl and merge to incorporate.
6. Add flour mixture into the bowl with oil mixture and merge to incorporate.
7. Fold in walnuts.
8. Place the bread mixture into the bread mold.
9. Bake in your oven for around 55 minutes.
10. Take off the bread mold from oven and put it onto cooling grid to cool for around 9-10 minutes.
11. Then turn the cake onto the cooling grid to allow it to reach room temperature before enjoying.

Ingredients

Three medium-sized bananas - Half C. unsweetened applesauce - Half C. Erythritol - Six tbsp. olive oil - Two large-sized eggs - One C. whole-wheat flour - Half C. ground flaxseed - One tsp. baking soda - One tsp. powdered cinnamon - One pinch of powdered allspice - Half tsp. salt - Quarter C. walnuts, roughly cut up

NUTRITIONAL VALUES : TOTAL CALORIES: 288; TOTAL CARBOHYDRATES: 32.8G; DIETARY FIBER: 4.2G; SUGARS: 18.3G; PROTEIN: 5.4G; TOTAL FAT: 2.1G; SATURATED FAT: 2.1G

Coconut Macaroons
With Dark Chocolate Drizzle

🕐 **Prep:** *20 mins*   ▣ **Cook:** *10 mins*   🛎 **Serves:** *12*

Directions

1. For preheating: set your oven at 350°F.
2. Lay out bakery paper onto a large-sized cookie tray.
3. Put coconut flour and remnant ingredients into the food mixer and whirl to incorporate thoroughly.
4. Divide the mixture up into tbsp.-size portions and place them onto the cookie tray.
5. Bake in your oven for around 7-10 minutes.
6. Take off from oven and let them cool for around 1 hour before enjoying.
7. For the chocolate drizzle: put chocolate into a microwave-safe dish and microwave on high setting for around 1½-2 minutes, blending after every 20 seconds.
8. Place the macaroons over a cooling rack and drizzle with chocolate.
9. Let it set for around 5 minutes before enjoying.

Ingredients

One tbsp. coconut flour - 1/8 tsp. sea salt - Quarter C. pure maple syrup - Two tbsp. coconut oil, melted - One tbsp. vanilla extract - One and half C. unsweetened coconut, shredded - 3 oz. unsweetened dark chocolate

NUTRITIONAL VALUES : TOTAL CALORIES: 125; TOTAL CARBOHYDRATES: 8.4G; DIETARY FIBER: 2.1G; SUGARS: 4.7G; PROTEIN: 1.4G; TOTAL FAT: 9.5G; SATURATED FAT: 7.3G

Greek Yogurt Berry
Parfait with Honey Drizzle

🕐 **Prep:** *10 mins*　　🍽 **Serves:** *1*

Directions

1. Put yogurt, vanilla extract and stevia into a bowl and whisk to form a perfectly silky mixture.
2. Place half of the yogurt into a serving dish.
3. Top the yogurt with half of the strawberries and walnuts.
4. Repeat the layers.
5. Drizzle the top with honey and enjoy right away.

Ingredients

Three quarters C. reduced-fat plain Greek yogurt - One tsp. vanilla extract - Two drops liquid stevia - Quarter C. fresh strawberries, hulled and slivered - Quarter C. walnuts, cut up - One tsp. honey

NUTRITIONAL VALUES : TOTAL CALORIES: 299; TOTAL CARBOHYDRATES: 19G; DIETARY FIBER: 2.9G; SUGARS: 2.6G; PROTEIN: 15.2G; TOTAL FAT: 18.7G; SATURATED FAT: 1.1G

Flourless Chocolate Brownies
With Raspberry Coulis

🕐 **Prep:** *15 mins*　　▣ **Cook:** *30 mins*　　🍽 **Serves:** *12*

Directions

1. For preheating: set your oven at 350ºF.
2. Line a large-sized baking pan with bakery paper.
3. Put the black beans and remnant ingredients except the cacao powder and cinnamon into the food mixer and whirl to incorporate thoroughly.
4. Shift the beans mixture into a large-sized bowl.
5. Put in cacao powder and cinnamon and merge to incorporate.
6. Now, shift the mixture into the baking pan and with the back of a spatula, smooth the top surface.
7. Bake in your oven for around 30 minutes.
8. In the meantime, for the raspberry coulis: in a small-sized cooking pot, put the raspberries, two tsp. Erythritol, cornstarch and two tbsp. of water on burner at moderate heat.
9. Cook the mixture until boiling.
10. Cook for around 5 minutes.
11. Take of the pan from burner and put it aside to cool slightly.
12. Take off the baking pan of brownies from oven and place onto the cooling grid to allow it to reach room temperature before enjoying.
13. Cut into 12 brownies.
14. Top with raspberry coulis and enjoy right away.

Ingredients

For the Brownies:
Two C. cooked black beans - Twelve Medjool dates, pitted and cut up - Two tbsp. almond butter - Two tbsp. quick rolled oats - Two tsp. vanilla extract - Quarter C. cacao powder - One tbsp. ground cinnamon

For the Raspberry Coulis:
One and half C. fresh raspberries, halved - Two tbsp. Erythritol - Three tsp. cornstarch - One third C. water

NUTRITIONAL VALUES : TOTAL CALORIES: 190; TOTAL CARBOHYDRATES: 36.2G; DIETARY FIBER: 8.3G; SUGARS: 11G; PROTEIN: 8.6G; TOTAL FAT: 2.5G; SATURATED FAT: 0.5G

Baked Pear Halves with Warm Spiced
Honey Glaze

🕐 **Prep:** *15 mins*   📲 **Cook:** *26 mins*   🍽 **Serves:** *4*

Directions

1. For preheating: set your oven at 375°F.
2. Lay out bakery paper onto a baking tray.
3. Carefully cut a small-sized sliver off the underside of each pear half.
4. Lay out the pear halves onto the baking tray, cut side upwards and sprinkle with cinnamon.
5. Put the maple syrup and vanilla extract into a small-sized bowl and whisk thoroughly.
6. Reserve about two tbsp. of the maple syrup mixture.
7. Place the remnant maple syrup mixture over the pears.
8. Bake in your oven for around 24-25 minutes.
9. Take off the baking tray of pears from oven and immediately drizzle with the reserved maple syrup mixture.
10. Enjoy moderately hot.

Ingredients

4 pears, halved and cored - Quarter tsp. powdered cinnamon - Half C. honey - One tsp. pure vanilla extract

NUTRITIONAL VALUES : TOTAL CALORIES: 227; TOTAL CARBOHYDRATES: 58.5G; DIETARY FIBER: 6.6G; SUGARS: 44G; PROTEIN: 0.8G; TOTAL FAT: 0.4G; SATURATED FAT: 0G

Sugar-Free Key Lime Pie
With Almond Crust

⏱ **Prep:** *20 mins*　🍲 **Cook:** *20 mins*　🍽 **Serves:** *8*

Directions

1. For preheating: set your oven at 400°F.
2. For crust: put almond flour and remnant ingredients into a medium-sized bowl and merge to incorporate thoroughly.
3. With your hands, knead the dough for around 1 minute.
4. Make a ball from the dough.
5. Lay out the dough ball between two wax paper and then roll it into 1/8-inch thick round.
6. Put the dough into a 9-inch pie dish.
7. With your hands press gently into the base and along the sides of the pie dish.
8. Now, prick the bottom and sides of crust with a fork at many places.
9. Bake in your oven for around 9-10 minutes.
10. Take off from oven and place the crust onto the cooling grid to allow it to reach room temperature.
11. Now, set your oven at 350°F.
12. For filling: in the food mixer, put coconut milk, Erythritol, heavy cream, xanthan gum, guar gum and stevia and whirl to incorporate thoroughly.
13. Add egg yolks and lime juice and whirl to incorporate thoroughly.
14. Spread the filling mixture over crust.
15. Bake in your oven for around 9-10 minutes.
16. Take off the pie dish from oven and place onto the cooling grid for around 10-12 minutes.
17. Freeze for around 3-4 hours before enjoying.

Ingredients

For Crust:
Half C. almond flour - Half C. coconut flour, sifted - Quarter C. Erythritol - Quarter C. butter, melted - Two eggs - Quarter tsp. salt

For Filling:
Three quarters C. unsweetened coconut milk - Half C. Erythritol - Quarter C. heavy cream - Two tsp. xanthan gum - One tsp. guar gum - Quarter tsp. powdered stevia - Three egg yolks - Half C. key lime juice - Two tbsp. unsweetened dried coconut

NUTRITIONAL VALUES : TOTAL CALORIES: 231; TOTAL CARBOHYDRATES: 9.2G; DIETARY FIBER: 5.2G; SUGARS: 1G; PROTEIN: 5.6G; TOTAL FAT: 19.8G; SATURATED FAT: 11.3G

Blueberry Cobbler

🕐 **Prep:** *10 mins*   🍲 **Cook:** *40 mins*   🍽 **Serves:** *4*

Directions

1. For preheating: set your oven at 3oo°F.
2. Lightly spray an 8x8-inch baking pan.
3. Put flour and remnant ingredients except for blackberries into a large-sized bowl and merge to incorporate thoroughly.
4. Place blackberries in the bottom of baking pan.
5. Spread flour mixture over blackberries.
6. Bake in your oven for 35-40 minutes.
7. Enjoy moderately hot.

Ingredients

Quarter C. coconut flour - Quarter C. arrowroot flour - Three quarters tsp. baking soda - Two tbsp. coconut oil, melted - Quarter C. banana, peel removed and mashed - Half tbsp. fresh lemon juice - Three tbsp. water - One and half C. fresh blueberries

NUTRITIONAL VALUES : TOTAL CALORIES: 99; TOTAL CARBOHYDRATES: 8.9G; DIETARY FIBER: 3.5G; SUGARS: 3.9G; PROTEIN: 1.3G; TOTAL FAT: 7.3G; SATURATED FAT: 6.1G

Spinach & Avocado
Sorbet

🕐 **Prep:** *15 mins*   🍽 **Serves:** *4*

Directions

1. Put spinach and remnant ingredients into a mixer and whirl to form a creamy and smooth mixture.
2. Shift the mixture into an ice-cream machine and whirl as per the instruction provided by the manufacturer.
3. Shift the sorbet mixture into a freezer-safe container and seal it tightly.
4. Shift the container of sorbet into your freezer for around 4-5 hours before enjoying.

Ingredients

Three C. fresh spinach, torn - One tbsp. fresh basil leaves - Half of avocado, peel removed, pitted and cut up - Three quarters C. almond milk - Twenty drops liquid stevia - One tsp. almonds, cut up very finely - One tsp. vanilla extract - One C. ice cubes

NUTRITIONAL VALUES : TOTAL CALORIES: 166; TOTAL CARBOHYDRATES: 5.7G; DIETARY FIBER: 3.2G; SUGARS: 1.9G; PROTEIN: 2.3G; TOTAL FAT: 16G; SATURATED FAT: 10.6G

Apple Crisp

🕐 **Prep:** *15 mins*   📷 **Cook:** *20 mins*   🍽 **Serves:** *10*

Directions

1. For preheating: set your oven at 300ºF.
2. Put all filling ingredients into a large-sized baking pan and gently blend to incorporate.
3. Put all topping ingredients into a medium-sized bowl and merge to incorporate thoroughly.
4. Place the topping over the filling mixture.
5. Bake in your oven for around 20 minutes.
6. Enjoy moderately hot.

Ingredients

For the Filling:
Two large-sized apples, peel removed, cored and cut up - Two tbsp. fresh apple juice - Two tbsp. water - Quarter tsp. powdered cinnamon

For the Topping:
Half C. gluten-free quick rolled oats - Two tbsp. walnuts, cut up - Quarter C. unsweetened coconut flakes - Half tsp. powdered cinnamon - Quarter C. water

NUTRITIONAL VALUES : TOTAL CALORIES: 93; TOTAL CARBOHYDRATES: 16.1G; DIETARY FIBER: 2.3G; SUGARS: 9.7G; PROTEIN: 1.4G; TOTAL FAT: 3G; SATURATED FAT: 1.5G

Lemon Soufflé

🕐 **Prep:** *15 mins*   📷 **Cook:** *20 mins*   🍽 **Serves:** *4*

Directions

1. For preheating: set your oven at 375ºF.
2. Spray 4 ramekins with oil mist.
3. Put egg whites into a clean glass bowl and whisk to form them foamy.
4. Add two tbsp. of Erythritol and whisk to form stiff peaks.
5. In another bowl, put ricotta cheese, egg yolks and remnant Erythritol and whisk to incorporate thoroughly.
6. Now, place the lemon juice and zest and merge to incorporate thoroughly.
7. Put in poppy seeds and vanilla extract and merge to incorporate thoroughly.
8. Put whipped egg whites into the bowl of ricotta mixture and gently blend to incorporate.
9. Place the ricotta mixture into ramekins.
10. Bake in your oven for around 20 minutes.
11. Take off the ramekins from oven and enjoy right away.

Ingredients

Olive oil mist - Two large-sized eggs (whites and yolks separated) - Quarter C. Erythritol, divided - One C. ricotta cheese - One tbsp. lemon juice - Two tsp. lemon zest, grated finely - One tsp. poppy seeds - One tsp. vanilla extract

NUTRITIONAL VALUES : TOTAL CALORIES: 130; TOTAL CARBOHYDRATES: 4G; DIETARY FIBER: 0.2G; SUGARS: 0.8G; PROTEIN: 10.4G; TOTAL FAT: 7.7G; SATURATED FAT: 1.7G

Cool Cucumber
Mint Infusion

🕐 **Prep:** *10 mins*   🍽 **Serves:** *3*

Directions

1. In a large-sized glass jar, place lemon, cucumber and mint leaves and pour water on top.
2. Cover the jar with a lid and shift into your refrigerator for around 2-4 hours before enjoying.

Ingredients

Two lemons, slivered
One cucumber, slivered
Two tbsp. fresh mint leaves
Six C. water

NUTRITIONAL VALUES : TOTAL CALORIES: 41; TOTAL CARBOHYDRATES: 10.4G; DIETARY FIBER: 2.3G; SUGARS: 6.8G; PROTEIN: 1.1G; TOTAL FAT: 0.2G; SATURATED FAT: 0G

Strawberry
Basil Iced Tea

🕐 **Prep:** *15 mins*   📷 **Cook:** *10 mins*   🍽 **Serves:** *8*

Directions

1. In a medium-sized cooking pot, put four C. of water on burner at moderate-high heat.
2. Cook the water until boiling.
3. Take of the pan of water from burner and add in the tea bags.
4. Let the tea steep for around 5 minutes.
5. Place the strawberries into a large-sized bowl.
6. In a small-sized cooking pot, put the remnant water and Erythritol on burner at moderate heat.
7. Cook the water until boiling, blending all the time.
8. Take off from burner and merge in basil.
9. Let it steep for around 9-10 minutes.
10. Strain the basil water over strawberries and then discard basil.
11. Put it aside to cool for around 25 minutes.
12. Place the strawberries with syrup and tea into a pitcher.
13. Shift into your refrigerator to chill.
14. Enjoy over ice.

Ingredients

Five C. water, divided - Eight black-tea bags - One lb. fresh strawberries, hulled and halved - Three quarters C. Erythritol - One C. fresh basil - Ice, for serving

NUTRITIONAL VALUES : TOTAL CALORIES: 19; TOTAL CARBOHYDRATES: 4.4G; DIETARY FIBER: 1.2G; SUGARS: 2.8G; PROTEIN: 0.5G; TOTAL FAT: 0.2G; SATURATED FAT: 0G

Creamy Chia Seed
& Berry Smoothie

🕐 **Prep:** *10 mins* 　　🍽 **Serves:** *2*

Directions

1. Put berries and remnant ingredients into a high-power mixer and whirl to form a creamy smoothie.
2. Enjoy right away.

Ingredients

One and half C. fresh berries - One tbsp. chia seeds - One and half C. unsweetened coconut milk - Quarter C. ice cubes

NUTRITIONAL VALUES : TOTAL CALORIES: 108; TOTAL CARBOHYDRATES: 15.8G; DIETARY FIBER: 5.8G; SUGARS: 7.5G; PROTEIN: 1.5G; TOTAL FAT: 4.6G; SATURATED FAT: 3.1G

Iced Golden
Turmeric Latte

🕐 **Prep:** *10 mins* 　　🍽 **Serves:** *2*

Directions

1. Put almond milk and remnant ingredients into a cocktail shaker.
2. Shake the mixture thoroughly.
3. Pour the latte over ice into two serving glasses and enjoy right away.

Ingredients

Two-three C. unsweetened almond milk - Three tbsp. maple syrup - One and half tsp. powdered turmeric - Quarter tsp. powdered cinnamon - Quarter tsp. powdered ginger - One pinch of powdered cardamom - One pinch of powdered black pepper - Quarter tsp. vanilla extract

NUTRITIONAL VALUES : TOTAL CALORIES: 149; TOTAL CARBOHYDRATES: 30G; DIETARY FIBER: 2G; SUGARS: 25G; PROTEIN: 1G; TOTAL FAT: 3G; SATURATED FAT: 1G

Raspberry Lemonade

🕐 **Prep:** *10 mins*   🍽 **Serves:** *6*

Directions

1. Place raspberries into a large-sized pitcher.
2. Put in lemon juice, water and stevia and merge to incorporate.
3. Pour into glasses over ice and enjoy right away.

Ingredients

Two and half C. frozen raspberries - Three quarters C. fresh lemon juice - Seven C. cold water - Thirty drops liquid stevia - Ice, as desired

NUTRITIONAL VALUES : TOTAL CALORIES: 115; TOTAL CARBOHYDRATES: 27.9G; DIETARY FIBER: 4.7G; SUGARS: 23.3G; PROTEIN: 1G; TOTAL FAT: 0.4G; SATURATED FAT: 0.3G

Peach Ginger
Green Tea Cooler

🕐 **Prep:** *15 mins*   🍽 **Serves:** *6*

Directions

1. Put peach slices and teabags into a cooking pot.
2. Pour boiling water on top and steep for around 5 minutes.
3. Strain the tea into a pitcher, reserving the peaches.
4. Add the honey and lemon juice into the pitcher and merge to incorporate.
5. Let the tea cool thoroughly.
6. Then Shift into your refrigerator the tea to chill.
7. Reserve the peaches in refrigerator.
8. Place ice and reserved peach slices into the serving glasses.
9. Top with chilled tea and mint.
10. Enjoy chilled.

Ingredients

3 ripe peaches, pitted and slivered - 6 green tea teabags - 6 C. boiling water - 2 tbsp. honey - 2 tbsp. lemon juice - 2-3 fresh mint sprigs

NUTRITIONAL VALUES : TOTAL CALORIES: 52; TOTAL CARBOHYDRATES: 12.9G; DIETARY FIBER: 1.2G; SUGARS: 12.9G; PROTEIN: 0.8G; TOTAL FAT: 0.2G; SATURATED FAT: 0G

Almond Joy
Protein Shake

🕐 **Prep:** *10 mins*   🍽 **Serves:** *2*

Directions

1. Add almonds and remnant ingredients into a high-power mixer and whirl to form a creamy shake.
2. Enjoy right away.

Ingredients

Half C. almonds, cut up - One scoop unsweetened protein powder - Quarter tsp. vanilla extract - Three-four drops liquid stevia - One and half C. unsweetened almond milk - Quarter C. ice cubes

NUTRITIONAL VALUES : TOTAL CALORIES: 227; TOTAL CARBOHYDRATES: 6.7G; DIETARY FIBER: 3.7G; SUGARS: 1.1G; PROTEIN: 18.5G; TOTAL FAT: 15G; SATURATED FAT: 1.1G

Mixed Berry
Detox Water

🕐 **Prep:** *10 mins*   🍽 **Serves:** *3*

Directions

1. In a large-sized glass jar, place berries, lemon and mint leaves and pour water on top.
2. Cover the jar with a lid and shift into your refrigerator for around 2-4 hours before enjoying.

Ingredients

One C. fresh mixed berries, slivered - 1 lemon, slivered - One tbsp. fresh mint leaves - 6 C. water

NUTRITIONAL VALUES : TOTAL CALORIES: 18; TOTAL CARBOHYDRATES: 4.3G; DIETARY FIBER: 1.2G; SUGARS: 2.5G; PROTEIN: 0.4G; TOTAL FAT: 0.2G; SATURATED FAT: 0G

Mocha Iced Coffee
With Coconut Milk

🕐 **Prep:** *10 mins*   🍽 **Serves:** *2*

Directions

1. Put coffee and remnant ingredients into a high-power mixer and pulse to form a perfectly silky mixture.
2. Enjoy right away.

Ingredients

Two C. strong brewed, chilled coffee - Half C. unsweetened almond milk - Two tbsp. unsweetened cocoa powder - One tsp. chocolate liquid stevia - Half C. ice cubes

NUTRITIONAL VALUES : TOTAL CALORIES: 25; TOTAL CARBOHYDRATES: 3.4G; DIETARY FIBER: 2G; SUGARS: 0.1G; PROTEIN: 1.6G; TOTAL FAT: 1.7G; SATURATED FAT: 0.5G

Apple Cinnamon
Hydration Drink

🕐 **Prep:** *10 mins*   🍽 **Serves:** *2*

Directions

1. Put apple slices and cinnamon sticks into a pitcher.
2. Fill pitcher with water and shift into your refrigerator for around 1 hour before enjoying.

Ingredients

Two apples, cored and slivered - Two cinnamon sticks - Water, as desired

NUTRITIONAL VALUES : TOTAL CALORIES: 98; TOTAL CARBOHYDRATES: 26G; DIETARY FIBER: 5G; SUGARS: 19G; PROTEIN: 1G; TOTAL FAT: 0G; SATURATED FAT: 0G

SAUCES & DRESSINGS

Classic Balsamic Vinaigrette
(Low-Sugar)

🕐 **Prep:** *10 mins*　　🍽 **Serves:** *8*

Directions

1. Put broth and remnant ingredients into a bowl and whisk to incorporate.
2. Vinaigrette is ready to use.

Ingredients

Half C. vegetable broth - **Quarter C. balsamic vinegar - Two tsp. Dijon mustard - One tbsp. maple syrup - One clove garlic finely cut up - Quarter tsp. salt - Quarter tsp. powdered black pepper - Two tbsp. olive oil**

NUTRITIONAL VALUES : TOTAL CALORIES: 41; TOTAL CARBOHYDRATES: 2.6G; DIETARY FIBER: 0.1G; SUGARS: 2.2G; PROTEIN: 0.4G; TOTAL FAT: 3.3G; SATURATED FAT: 0.5G

Creamy Avocado
Cilantro Dressing

🕐 **Prep:** *10 mins*　　🍽 **Serves:** *16*

Directions

1. Place avocado and remnant ingredients into a mixer and whirl to form a perfectly silky mixture.
2. Vinaigrette is ready to use.

Ingredients

Half of ripe avocado, peel removed and pitted - Three quarters C. fresh cilantro - Half C. fat-free plain yogurt - Two scallions, cut up - One clove garlic, quartered - One tbsp. lime juice - Half tsp. Erythritol - Half tsp. salt

NUTRITIONAL VALUES : TOTAL CALORIES: 16; TOTAL CARBOHYDRATES: 2G; DIETARY FIBER: 1G; SUGARS: 1G; PROTEIN: 1G; TOTAL FAT: 1G; SATURATED FAT: 0G

Tangy Lemon
Herb Marinade

🕐 **Prep:** *10 mins*   🍽 **Serves:** *4*

Directions

1. Place yogurt and remnant ingredients into small-sized bowl and stir with whisk to form a perfectly silky mixture.
2. Let it rest for around 30 minutes before enjoying.

Ingredients

Half C. plain reduced-fat yogurt - Two tbsp. fresh parsley, cut up - One clove garlic, finely cut up - Half tbsp. olive oil - Half tsp. lemon zest, finely cut up - Half tbsp. lemon juice - One tsp. dill weed - Quarter tsp. salt

NUTRITIONAL VALUES : TOTAL CALORIES: 36; TOTAL CARBOHYDRATES: 2.6G; DIETARY FIBER: 0.1G; SUGARS: 2.2G; PROTEIN: 1.7G; TOTAL FAT: 2.2G; SATURATED FAT: 0.5G

Roasted Red
Pepper & Garlic Aioli

🕐 **Prep:** *10 mins*   🍽 **Serves:** *10*

Directions

1. Put mayonnaise and remnant ingredients into the food mixer and whirl to form a perfectly silky mixture.
2. Shift the aioli into a bowl.
3. Shift into your refrigerator for around 30 minutes before enjoying.

Ingredients

Three quarters C. mayonnaise - Six cloves garlic, finely cut up - Two tbsp. fresh lemon juice - Half C. roasted red peppers, cut up - Two-three tbsp. fresh flat-leaf parsley - Quarter tsp. sea salt - One pinch of powdered black pepper

NUTRITIONAL VALUES : TOTAL CALORIES: 114; TOTAL CARBOHYDRATES: 1G; DIETARY FIBER: 0G; SUGARS: 2G; PROTEIN: 0G; TOTAL FAT: 12G; SATURATED FAT: 3.1G

Fresh Basil Pesto
(Nut-Free Version)

🕐 **Prep:** *15 mins*　　🍽 **Serves:** *8*

Directions

1. Put basil and remnant ingredients except the oil and cheese into the food mixer and whirl to form a perfectly silky mixture.
2. Slowly put in oil and cheese and whirl to form a perfectly silky mixture.
3. Enjoy right away.

Ingredients

One C. fresh basil leaves - Half C. fresh flat-leaf parsley leaves - Half C. fresh baby spinach - One large-sized clove garlic, peel removed - Three tbsp. sunflower seeds - One tsp. fresh lemon zest, grated - One pinch of salt and powdered black pepper - One and quarter C. olive oil - Half C. Parmesan cheese, grated finely

NUTRITIONAL VALUES : TOTAL CALORIES: 315; TOTAL CARBOHYDRATES: 1.6G; DIETARY FIBER: 0.5G; SUGARS: 0.2G; PROTEIN: 2.8G; TOTAL FAT: 34.9G; SATURATED FAT: 8.1G

Smoky Tomato
Barbecue Sauce

🕐 **Prep:** *10 mins*　　🍲 **Cook:** *25 mins*　　🍽 **Serves:** *16*

Directions

1. Put tomato sauce and remnant ingredients into a small-sized cooking pot on burner at moderate-low heat and merge to incorporate.
2. Cook the mixture until boiling.
3. Immediately turn the heat at low.
4. Cook with the cover for around 20 minutes.
5. Take off the pan of tomato sauce from burner.
6. Set the pan of sauce aside to cool before enjoying.

Ingredients

Two C. tomato sauce - One C. sugar-free Ketchup - Quarter C. apple cider vinegar - Two tbsp. butter - Three tbsp. simple barbecue spice blend - One tsp. liquid smoke - One tsp. stevia - One tsp. sea salt

NUTRITIONAL VALUES : TOTAL CALORIES: 35; TOTAL CARBOHYDRATES: 7.7G; DIETARY FIBER: 0.5G; SUGARS: 0.5G; PROTEIN: 0.7G; TOTAL FAT: 1.6G; SATURATED FAT: 0.9G

Zesty Dijon
Mustard Dressing

🕐 **Prep:** *10 mins*   🍽 **Serves:** *6*

Directions

1. Put mustard and remnant ingredients into a bowl and whisk to incorporate.
2. Dressing is ready to use.

Ingredients

Two tbsp. Dijon mustard - Two tbsp. olive oil - Two tbsp. apple cider vinegar - One tbsp. honey - One small-sized clove garlic, finely cut up - Salt and powdered black pepper, as desired

NUTRITIONAL VALUES : TOTAL CALORIES: 55; TOTAL CARBOHYDRATES: 3.2G; DIETARY FIBER: 0.2G; SUGARS: 2.9G; PROTEIN: 0.2G; TOTAL FAT: 4.9G; SATURATED FAT: 0.7G

Olive Tapenade
With Lemon Zest

🕐 **Prep:** *10 mins*   🍽 **Serves:** *16*

Directions

1. Put the olives and garlic into the food mixer and whirl to cut up finely.
2. Put in oil and parsley and whirl to incorporate thoroughly.
3. Shift the dip into a serving dish and enjoy right away.

Ingredients

Two C. Greek olives, pitted - Three cloves garlic, finely cut up - Three tbsp. olive oil - Two tsp. fresh parsley, finely cut up

NUTRITIONAL VALUES : TOTAL CALORIES: 43; TOTAL CARBOHYDRATES: 1.3G; DIETARY FIBER: 0.6G; SUGARS: 0G; PROTEIN: 0.2G; TOTAL FAT: 4.4G; SATURATED FAT: 0.1G

Roasted Garlic & Parmesan
Alfredo Sauce

🕐 **Prep:** *10 mins*   ▣ **Cook:** *10 mins*   🍽 **Serves:** *6*

Directions

1. Sizzle oil into a stainless steel cooking pot on burner at moderate-low heat.
2. Cook the garlic for around 1 minute.
3. Put in butter and let it melt.
4. Slowly whisk in flour to incorporate thoroughly.
5. Slowly add in 1 half C. of almond milk and merge to incorporate.
6. Immediately turn the heat at medium.
7. Cook for around 2-3 minutes, blending all the time.
8. Immediately turn the heat at low.
9. Add in the cheese and cook to melt thoroughly.
10. Blend in salt and pepper and take off from burner.
11. Enjoy right away.

Ingredients

Half tsp. olive oil - Four-five cloves garlic, finely cut up - Four tsp. unsalted butter - Four tsp. whole-wheat flour - One and three quarters C. unsweetened almond milk - Quarter C. reduced-fat cheddar cheese, shredded - One third C. reduced-fat Parmesan cheese, shredded - Two tbsp. reduced-fat Pecorino Romano chees - Salt and powdered black pepper, as desired

NUTRITIONAL VALUES : TOTAL CALORIES: 140; TOTAL CARBOHYDRATES: 4G; DIETARY FIBER: 1G; SUGARS: 0.3G; PROTEIN: 6G; TOTAL FAT: 11G; SATURATED FAT: 6G

Spicy Chipotle
Avocado Mayo

🕐 **Prep:** *10 mins*   🍽 **Serves:** *6*

Directions

1. Put yogurt and remnant ingredients into a mixer and pulse to form a perfectly silky mixture.
2. Enjoy right away.

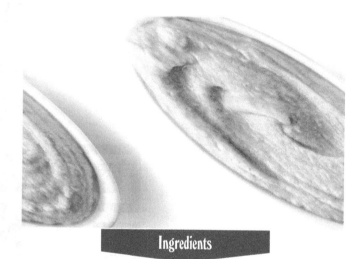

Ingredients

One C. fat-free plain Greek yogurt - One-two chipotle peppers in adobo sauce - Half of medium avocado, peel removed, pitted and cut up - One clove garlic - Quarter C. fresh cilantro leaves - One tbsp. lime juice - One-two tbsp. water - Quarter tsp. salt

NUTRITIONAL VALUES : TOTAL CALORIES: 68; TOTAL CARBOHYDRATES: 5.4G; DIETARY FIBER: 1.3G; SUGARS: 3.4G; PROTEIN: 2.6G; TOTAL FAT: 3.8G; SATURATED FAT: 1.1G

CONCLUSION

First and foremost, I want to express my sincere gratitude to you for taking an interest in this book. Your eagerness to learn about nutrition and managing your health is a wonderful step towards a better, more vibrant you. So, from the bottom of my heart, thank you for embarking on this journey with us.

I understand that all the information we've covered may sometimes feel like a lot to take in. It's like having a full plate of delicious food in front of you; you want to savor every bit, but it can be overwhelming. Remember, it's okay to take it one step at a time. Just like enjoying a good meal, savor each morsel of knowledge and apply it gradually to your life. Small-sized changes can lead to big improvements over time.

Life is full of distractions, just like a bustling market with tempting treats around every corner. It's easy to get sidetracked. But one of the most crucial aspects of this journey is staying focused. Think of it as keeping your eyes on the prize - your health and well-being.

And speaking of journey, remember that consistency is your loyal companion on this path. It's like the steady beat of a drum that keeps you moving forward. Consistency is the key to making positive changes stick. Whether it's in your diet, exercise routine, or other aspects of life, staying consistent will yield the best results.

So, as you move forward on your quest for a healthier and happier you, remember to take things one step at a time, stay focused and maintain that all-important consistency. You've got the knowledge and the will and that's a powerful combination. I believe in you and I'm excited to see the positive changes you'll make on this journey. Here's to your health and a brighter, more energetic future! Cheers to you!

HERE IS YOUR FREE GIFT!

SCAN HERE TO DOWNLOAD IT

30-DAY MEAL PLAN

WEEK 1

Day 1
- Breakfast: Wholesome Oat and Berry Bowl
- Snack: Roasted Chickpeas with Cumin and Paprika
- Lunch: Grilled Chicken Salad with Lettuce
- Dinner: Lemon Tilapia with Roasted Broccoli

Day 2
- Breakfast: Scrambled Tofu Veggie Delight
- Snack: Crunchy Veggie Sticks with Hummus Dip
- Lunch: Quinoa & Black Bean Bowl with Lime Dressing
- Dinner: Herb-Crusted Baked Salmon with Lemon Asparagus

Day 3
- Breakfast: Avocado & Tomato Whole-Wheat Toast
- Snack: Almond-Stuffed Medjool Dates
- Lunch: Tomato & Basil Whole Wheat Pasta Salad
- Dinner: Spaghetti Squash Primavera with Olive Oil Drizzle

Day 4
- Breakfast: Almond Butter & Banana Sandwich
- Snack: Unsweetened Cocoa-Dusted Almonds
- Lunch: Seared Tuna with Greens
- Dinner: Seared Cod with Tomato & Olives

Day 5
- Breakfast: Cinnamon Chia Seed Pudding
- Snack: Spicy Edamame with Garlic and Chili
- Lunch: Broccoli & Cauliflower Salad with Mustard Vinaigrette
- Dinner: Cilantro Lime Chicken with Zucchini Noodles

Day 6
- Breakfast: Veggie-Packed Omelette
- Snack: Cucumber and Tuna Salad Cups
- Lunch: Roast Beef & Arugula Sandwich
- Dinner: Rosemary Lamb Chops with Steamed Green Beans

Day 7
- Breakfast: Quinoa & Fruit Salad
- Snack: Savory Roasted Pumpkin Seeds
- Lunch: Hearty Vegetable & Barley Soup
- Dinner: Pesto & Mozzarella Stuffed Chicken Breasts

WEEK 2

Day 8
- Breakfast: Low-Sugar Blueberry Muffins
- Snack: Nutty No-Bake Energy Bites
- Lunch: Turkey & Avocado Spinach Wrap
- Dinner: Beef & Vegetable Kabobs with Tzatziki Sauce

Day 9
- Breakfast: Spinach & Mushroom Frittata
- Snack: Zesty Lemon & Herb Greek Yogurt Dip
- Lunch: Spiced Turkey & Vegetable Stuffed Peppers
- Dinner: Cajun Shrimp & Cauliflower Rice Bowl

Day 10
- Breakfast: Classic Egg Salad on Rye
- Snack: Oven-Baked Sweet Potato Chips
- Lunch: Spinach & Goat Cheese Stuffed Chicken Breast
- Dinner: Slow-Cooked Chicken Marsala

Day 11
- Breakfast: Poached Eggs with Avocado Salad
- Snack: Cheesy Kale Chips
- Lunch: Balsamic Glazed Grilled Portobello Mushrooms
- Dinner: Vegetarian Chili with Avocado & Sour Cream

Day 12
- Breakfast: Mixed Seed and Nut Porridge
- Snack: Avocado and Egg Salad Lettuce Wraps
- Lunch: Classic Caesar Salad with Grilled Shrimp
- Dinner: Honey Mustard Glazed Pork Chops with Apple Slaw

Day 13
- Breakfast: Zucchini & Walnut Bread
- Snack: Peanut Butter Celery Sticks
- Lunch: Ratatouille
- Dinner: Spicy Tofu with Veggies

Day 14
- Breakfast: Berries Yogurt Bowl
- Snack: Nuts & Dried Cranberry Mix
- Lunch: Tuna & Apple Sandwiches
- Dinner: Parmesan Crusted Tilapia with Broccoli

30-DAY MEAL PLAN

WEEK 3

Day 15
- Breakfast: Mixed Berry Smoothie with Kale
- Snack: Pumpkin Seed Clusters
- Lunch: Cold Sesame Noodle Salad with Veggies
- Dinner: Balsamic Glazed Beef Stir Fry with Mixed Veggies

Day 16
- Breakfast: Pumpkin Spice Overnight Oats
- Snack: Cherry Tomato & Mozzarella Skewers
- Lunch: Greek Salad with Grilled Chicken
- Dinner: Lemon Garlic Shrimp with Quinoa

Day 17
- Breakfast: Spinach, Feta & Tomato Scramble
- Snack: Lightly Salted Air-Popped Popcorn
- Lunch: Avocado & Chicken Salad with Lime Dressing
- Dinner: Grilled Salmon with Asparagus and Lemon Butter

Day 18
- Breakfast: Eggs & Cheese Breakfast Wrap
- Snack: Spiced Guacamole with Bell Pepper Dippers
- Lunch: Mediterranean Veggie Wrap
- Dinner: Chicken and Vegetable Stir-Fry

Day 19
- Breakfast: Nutty Granola with Unsweetened Almond Milk
- Snack: Fresh Fruit Salad with a Hint of Mint
- Lunch: Tuna Salad with Mixed Greens
- Dinner: Turkey Meatballs with Spaghetti Squash

Day 20
- Breakfast: Coconut & Almond Pancakes
- Snack: Jicama, Carrot and Apple Salad
- Lunch: Quinoa Stuffed Bell Peppers
- Dinner: Baked Cod with Lemon and Dill

Day 21
- Breakfast: Dark Chocolate Avocado Mousse
- Snack: Zesty Lime and Shrimp Skewers
- Lunch: Grilled Chicken Salad with Lettuce
- Dinner: Lemon Tilapia with Roasted Broccoli

WEEK 4

Day 22
- Breakfast: Berry Bliss Chia Seed Pudding
- Snack: Classic Deviled Eggs with a Twist
- Lunch: Quinoa & Black Bean Bowl with Lime Dressing
- Dinner: Herb-Crusted Baked Salmon with Lemon Asparagus

Day 23
- Breakfast: Light Vanilla Bean Panna Cotta with Berry Compote
- Snack: Carrot Sticks with Pesto
- Lunch: Tomato & Basil Whole Wheat Pasta Salad
- Dinner: Spaghetti Squash Primavera with Olive Oil Drizzle

Day 24
- Breakfast: Lemon Ricotta Almond Cake
- Snack: Tomato Bruschetta with Fresh Basil & Balsamic Reduction
- Lunch: Seared Tuna with Greens
- Dinner: Seared Cod with Tomato & Olives

Day 25
- Breakfast: Spiced Applesauce Cake
- Snack: Spinach & Feta Stuffed Mushrooms
- Lunch: Broccoli & Cauliflower Salad with Mustard Vinaigrette
- Dinner: Cilantro Lime Chicken with Zucchini Noodles

Day 26
- Breakfast: No-Bake Peanut Butter Protein Balls
- Snack: Mini Turkey Lettuce Wraps
- Lunch: Turkey & Avocado Spinach Wrap
- Dinner: Beef & Vegetable Kabobs with Tzatziki Sauce

Day 27
- Breakfast: Cinnamon Swirl Baked Donuts
- Snack: Crispy Baked Cauliflower Bites with Garlic Yogurt Dip
- Lunch: Spiced Turkey & Vegetable Stuffed Peppers
- Dinner: Cajun Shrimp & Cauliflower Rice Bowl

Day 28
- Breakfast: Berries Yogurt Bowl
- Snack: Nuts & Dried Cranberry Mix
- Lunch: Tuna & Apple Sandwiches
- Dinner: Parmesan Crusted Tilapia with Broccoli

WEEKLY SHOPPING LIST - WEEK 1

Fruits, Vegetables & Legumes
- Strawberries
- Blueberries
- Cherry tomatoes
- Fresh asparagus
- Lemon
- Avocado
- Tomato
- Red onion
- Cucumber
- Medjool dates
- Almonds (for stuffing dates)
- Broccoli
- Cauliflower
- Zucchini
- Green beans
- Pumpkin seeds
- Garlic
- Bell peppers (various colors)
- Spinach
- Mixed greens (for salads)
- Edamame
- Lime
- Fresh herbs (basil, cilantro, parsley, rosemary, dill, etc.)

Dairy & Eggs
- Egg whites
- Tofu
- Greek yogurt
- Mozzarella cheese
- Feta cheese
- Parmesan cheese

Grains, Nuts & Seeds
- Gluten-free quick-cooking oats
- Whole wheat bread
- Quinoa
- Whole wheat pasta
- Spaghetti squash
- Almond butter
- Chia seeds
- Almonds (for snacking)
- Whole wheat tortillas or pita pockets

Meat, Fish & Seafood
- Chicken (breasts or whole)
- Tilapia fillets
- Salmon fillets
- Tuna (fresh or canned)
- Cod fillets
- Lamb chops

Pantry Items
- Olive oil
- Various spices (cumin, paprika, cayenne, turmeric, cinnamon, etc.)
- Honey
- Balsamic vinegar
- Mustard
- Marinara sauce
- Coconut oil
- Sea salt
- Black pepper

Others
- Hummus (for dipping)
- Lemon juice
- Coconut milk (optional for smoothies or drinks)

WEEKLY SHOPPING LIST - WEEK 2

Fruits & Vegetables
- Blueberries (for Low-Sugar Blueberry Muffins)
- Avocado (for Turkey & Avocado Spinach Wrap, Poached Eggs with Avocado Salad, Vegetarian Chili with Avocado & Sour Cream)
- Spinach (for Spinach & Mushroom Frittata, Turkey & Avocado Spinach Wrap, Classic Caesar Salad with Grilled Shrimp)
- Mushrooms (for Spinach & Mushroom Frittata)
- Bell Peppers (for Spiced Turkey & Vegetable Stuffed Peppers)
- Cauliflower (for Cajun Shrimp & Cauliflower Rice Bowl)
- Sweet Potato (for Oven-Baked Sweet Potato Chips)
- Zucchini (for Zucchini & Walnut Bread)
- Lettuce (for Avocado and Egg Salad Lettuce Wraps)
- Kale (for Cheesy Kale Chips)
- Portobello Mushrooms (for Balsamic Glazed Grilled Portobello Mushrooms)
- Cucumber (for Beef & Vegetable Kabobs with Tzatziki Sauce)
- Apple (for Honey Mustard Glazed Pork Chops with Apple Slaw, Tuna & Apple Sandwiches)
- Broccoli (for Parmesan Crusted Tilapia with Broccoli)

Dairy & Eggs
- Eggs (for Classic Egg Salad on Rye, Spinach & Mushroom Frittata, Poached Eggs with Avocado Salad)
- Goat Cheese (for Spinach & Goat Cheese Stuffed Chicken Breast)
- Greek Yogurt (for Zesty Lemon & Herb Greek Yogurt Dip)
- Feta Cheese (for Classic Caesar Salad with Grilled Shrimp)
- Sour Cream (for Vegetarian Chili with Avocado & Sour Cream)

Grains, Nuts & Seeds
- Rye Bread (for Classic Egg Salad on Rye)
- Almond Flour (for Zucchini & Walnut Bread)
- Walnuts (for Zucchini & Walnut Bread)
- Mixed Seeds (for Mixed Seed and Nut Porridge)
- Nuts & Dried Cranberries (for Nuts & Dried Cranberry Mix)

Meat, Fish & Seafood
- Turkey (for Turkey & Avocado Spinach Wrap, Spiced Turkey & Vegetable Stuffed Peppers)
- Beef (for Beef & Vegetable Kabobs with Tzatziki Sauce)
- Shrimp (for Cajun Shrimp & Cauliflower Rice Bowl, Classic Caesar Salad with Grilled Shrimp)
- Chicken Breast (for Spinach & Goat Cheese Stuffed Chicken Breast, Slow-Cooked Chicken Marsala)
- Pork Chops (for Honey Mustard Glazed Pork Chops with Apple Slaw)
- Tilapia (for Parmesan Crusted Tilapia with Broccoli)

Pantry Items
- Olive Oil
- Balsamic Vinegar
- Spices (e.g., Salt, Pepper, Garlic Powder, Cinnamon, etc.)
- Stevia or other sweeteners
- Tzatziki Sauce ingredients (if making from scratch)

Others
- Tofu (for Spicy Tofu with Veggies)
- Ratatouille ingredients (for Ratatouille dish)
- Peanut Butter (for Peanut Butter Celery Sticks)

Fruits & Vegetables
- Mixed Berries (for Mixed Berry Smoothie with Kale)
- Kale (for Mixed Berry Smoothie with Kale)
- Pumpkin (for Pumpkin Spice Overnight Oats)
- Cherry Tomatoes (for Cherry Tomato & Mozzarella Skewers)
- Avocado (for Avocado & Chicken Salad with Lime Dressing, Dark Chocolate Avocado Mousse)
- Spinach (for Spinach, Feta & Tomato Scramble)
- Bell Peppers (for Spiced Guacamole with Bell Pepper Dippers, Quinoa Stuffed Bell Peppers)
- Asparagus (for Grilled Salmon with Asparagus and Lemon Butter)
- Lemon (for Lemon Garlic Shrimp with Quinoa, Grilled Salmon with Asparagus and Lemon Butter, Baked Cod with Lemon and Dill, Lemon Tilapia with Roasted Broccoli)
- Jicama, Carrot, Apple (for Jicama, Carrot and Apple Salad)
- Broccoli (for Lemon Tilapia with Roasted Broccoli)
- Fresh Fruit (for Fresh Fruit Salad with a Hint of Mint)

Dairy & Eggs
- Feta Cheese (for Spinach, Feta & Tomato Scramble)
- Mozzarella Cheese (for Cherry Tomato & Mozzarella Skewers)
- Eggs (for Eggs & Cheese Breakfast Wrap, Spinach, Feta & Tomato Scramble)

Grains, Nuts & Seeds
- Oats (for Pumpkin Spice Overnight Oats)
- Granola (for Nutty Granola with Unsweetened Almond Milk)
- Quinoa (for Lemon Garlic Shrimp with Quinoa, Quinoa Stuffed Bell Peppers)
- Almonds (for Coconut & Almond Pancakes)

Meat, Fish & Seafood
- Beef (for Balsamic Glazed Beef Stir Fry with Mixed Veggies)
- Chicken (for Greek Salad with Grilled Chicken, Avocado & Chicken Salad with Lime Dressing, Chicken and Vegetable Stir-Fry)
- Shrimp (for Lemon Garlic Shrimp with Quinoa, Zesty Lime and Shrimp Skewers)
- Salmon (for Grilled Salmon with Asparagus and Lemon Butter)
- Turkey (for Turkey Meatballs with Spaghetti Squash)
- Cod (for Baked Cod with Lemon and Dill)
- Tilapia (for Lemon Tilapia with Roasted Broccoli)

Pantry Items
- Sesame Seeds (for Cold Sesame Noodle Salad with Veggies)
- Balsamic Vinegar (for Balsamic Glazed Beef Stir Fry with Mixed Veggies)
- Spices (e.g., Salt, Pepper, Garlic Powder, Dill, etc.)
- Dark Chocolate (for Dark Chocolate Avocado Mousse)
- Coconut Flour (for Coconut & Almond Pancakes)

Others
- Pumpkin Seeds (for Pumpkin Seed Clusters)
- Air-Popped Popcorn (for Lightly Salted Air-Popped Popcorn)
- Guacamole ingredients (for Spiced Guacamole with Bell Pepper Dippers)
- Unsweetened Almond Milk (for Nutty Granola with Unsweetened Almond Milk)

Fruits & Vegetables

- Mixed Berries (for Berry Bliss Chia Seed Pudding)
- Lemons (for Herb-Crusted Baked Salmon with Lemon Asparagus, Lemon Ricotta Almond Cake)
- Carrots (for Carrot Sticks with Pesto)
- Tomatoes (for Tomato Bruschetta, Seared Cod with Tomato & Olives, Tomato & Basil Whole Wheat Pasta Salad)
- Fresh Basil (for Tomato Bruschetta, Tomato & Basil Whole Wheat Pasta Salad)
- Zucchini (for Cilantro Lime Chicken with Zucchini Noodles)
- Broccoli (for Broccoli & Cauliflower Salad with Mustard Vinaigrette)
- Cauliflower (for Broccoli & Cauliflower Salad with Mustard Vinaigrette)
- Spinach (for Turkey & Avocado Spinach Wrap)
- Bell Peppers (for Spiced Turkey & Vegetable Stuffed Peppers)
- Onions (for various recipes)
- Garlic (for various recipes)

Dairy & Eggs

- Eggs (for Classic Deviled Eggs with a Twist, various breakfast recipes)
- Greek Yogurt (for various recipes)
- Cheese (various types as required by recipes)

Grains, Nuts & Seeds

- Quinoa (for Quinoa & Black Bean Bowl with Lime Dressing)
- Whole Wheat Pasta (for Tomato & Basil Whole Wheat Pasta Salad)
- Almonds (for Lemon Ricotta Almond Cake)
- Chia Seeds (for Berry Bliss Chia Seed Pudding)
- Oats (for No-Bake Peanut Butter Protein Balls)

Meat, Fish & Seafood

- Salmon (for Herb-Crusted Baked Salmon with Lemon Asparagus)
- Tuna (for Seared Tuna with Greens)
- Cod (for Seared Cod with Tomato & Olives)
- Turkey (for Turkey & Avocado Spinach Wrap, Spiced Turkey & Vegetable Stuffed Peppers)
- Beef (for Beef & Vegetable Kabobs with Tzatziki Sauce)

Pantry Items

- Olive Oil (for various recipes)
- Balsamic Vinegar (for Tomato Bruschetta with Fresh Basil & Balsamic Reduction)
- Spices (such as Salt, Pepper, Cumin, etc.)
- Honey (for various recipes)
- Peanut Butter (for No-Bake Peanut Butter Protein Balls)

Others

- Vanilla Beans (for Light Vanilla Bean Panna Cotta with Berry Compote)
- Cocoa Powder (for Chocolate-based recipes)
- Baking Ingredients (such as flour, baking powder, etc. for baking recipes)

Made in the USA
Las Vegas, NV
08 February 2024

85517302R00063